THE NEW FOODS

HENRY HOLT and COMPANY

NEW YORK

THE NEW FOODS

A SHOPPER'S GUIDE WITH RECIPES

CAMILLE CUSUMANO

To my mother and father,
who gave me a venturesome palate

Published by Henry Holt and Company, Inc.,
115 West 18th Street, New York, New York 10011.
Published in Canada by Fitzhenry & Whiteside Limited,
195 Allstate Parkway, Markham, Ontario L3R 4T8.

Library of Congress Cataloging-in-Publication Data
Cusumano, Camille.
The new foods.
Includes index.
1. Cookery.   2. Food.   I. Title.
TX714.C87   1989   641   88-13283
ISBN 0-8050-0308-8

First Edition

Designed by Claire M. Naylon
Illustrations by Madeline Sorel
Printed in the United States of America
1 3 5 7 9 10 8 6 4 2

CONTENTS

Contents

Chili Peppers   135

Mushrooms   144

Grains, Beans, Nuts, and Seeds   155

Herbs and Spices 194

Specialty Vinegars and Oils   214

Flavors from the East   221

Sea Vegetables   232

ACKNOWLEDGMENTS

I am grateful to Jan Bresnick, who led me to Peter Elek, who led me to this book. Every food writer needs a room and a kitchen of her own. I am grateful to my grandmother, Jennie Catalano, who was responsible for a haven in which to produce this book and its recipes. Thanks for their expertise and assistance: Bill Schaefer of J. R. Brooks & Son, Inc.; Chris Rollins of Preston B. Bird and Mary Heinlein Fruit & Spice Park; Carol Bowman-Williams of Frieda's Finest; herbalist Dave Winston; wild-food expert John Gottfried; John Schmidt of Great Eastern Sun.

PREFACE

Americans have begun to outgrow what James Beard once dubbed the "six-year-old palate," referring to an infantile aversion to adventurous dining.

Indeed, all around us are signs that we Americans have been ready for a landmark change in our diets. Witness the steady flourish of restaurants, the growing interest in ethnic cuisines, and, not least of all, the supermarket's exotic produce section—a driving force for this book.

One wholesale produce distributor, Frieda Caplan, sends bushels of unusual and exotic fruits and vegetables to every corner of the nation daily. Frieda's freshly picked passion fruit, cherimoyas, and tomatillos, and many other fruits and vegetables all satisfy the growing demand for new and unusual foods.

Food journalists, noting Americans' receptivity to the adventurous eating trends, have dubbed the eighties the decade of "upscale pizza and pasta." This means anything from capers to Swiss chard may enhance once commonplace fare.

There's no doubt about it. An open and innovative spirit in cooking is gaining momentum. And the availability and variety of ingredients from around the world is growing, too, with jet-age swiftness. We eat only 100 to 150 of the world's 80,000 edible plants available to us, says Frieda Caplan, but we are clamoring for more and more of the untried.

As the world's food markets come to us with a magnificent and impressive array of colors, shapes, textures, and smells, we are staggered as well as seduced. "Ingredients are the fundamentals of cookery and every cook who hopes to excel should know about them," writes Tom Stobart in the *Cook's Encyclopedia* (Harper & Row, 1981).

That aphorism is basically the reason for this book.

Whether it's a rose-blushed prickly pear, a crotchety shiitake mushroom, or a bouquet of pungent arugula, we want to know all about these new ingredients. The list of alternative names, the description of proper color, texture, taste, aroma, and other characteristics are useful guides to cooking with these ingredients. Thus, I have tried to include all this information for each ingredient.

In addition, knowing how an item has been traditionally used—in its native and other cuisines—will stimulate your own imagination. Where to find each item, its storage and its keeping properties, and how to prepare it are important fundamentals included here, too.

I hope *The New Foods* helps you to know a little more about our expanding world of good and unusual ingredients. I hope, too, that it satisfies your curiosity (as writing it did mine), so that in the marketplace, you don't feel like Alice in Wonderland. Knowing that the odd-shaped squash called chayote requires only a simple steaming or sautéing makes it a lot less intimidating. To discover the added dimension of a pinch of crushed fresh cilantro in Mexican burritos is to make your home cooking all the more authentic. As a home cook, you'll feel confident knowing what to look for, how to store these foods, and how to assimilate them into our American eating culture.

I can't say it any better than did revered novelist and food writer M. F. K. Fisher: "The more you know about flavors, textures, and cooking food, the better it is."

FRUITS

Nothing is more versatile than fruit. It is correct in every course of a meal—from the appetizer to the dessert and everything in between. It's a wholesome fresh food, served simply as a snack. We also enjoy meat, poultry, and seafood entrées more and more with the sweet or tart embellishments of a fruit. Containing up to 85 percent water, most fruits translate easily into satisfying beverages, too. Cooks have welcomed the new exotic fruits in this section with the same range of imagination given to our favorite standbys. No doubt, once these fruits become familiar to you, you'll stretch their uses, too.

From a health standpoint, most fruits make a generously nourishing contribution to your diet. Most are high in fiber and along with vegetables are our most prolific source of vitamins A and C, which, according to the National Institutes of Health, are anticancer vitamins. Many fruits contribute some B vitamins and good amounts of important minerals such as potassium and phosphorus.

The sugar in fruits, fructose, is a much more reliable source of fast energy than the quickly metabolized sugar of a candy bar.

You should wash all fruit you don't peel, to remove any pesticide residues; but avoid soaking fruit, as this diminishes flavor. Selection and storage information given here is intended to assist you in getting specimens that provide peak pleasure. As with familiar fruits, repeated experience with these fruits may prove to be your best guide in what to choose and what to pass over.

Asian Pear (Apple Pear)

We have our great influx of Chinese immigrants during California's gold rush to thank for the appearance of the Asian pear in this country. They propagated the seeds all along streams of the Mother Lode country, giving us a perennial type of gold. For years only Asian growers enjoyed this fruit, which melds the slurping juiciness of a pear with the crisp crunchiness of an apple, whence its common appellation *apple pear*. However, the ambiguous fruit is not a cross between the two, but has its own identity in the pear genus *Pyrus*. California nurseries are now eagerly nurturing the pear's increasing popularity.

The Oriental name *sha li* means "sand pear," no doubt referring to the meltingly grainy texture of the ripe fruit. Other nomenclature for Asian pears includes *Nihon nashi* and *salad pear*, and *Chinese* or *Japanese pears*. But in the marketplace they are most apt to be called apple pears. The different varieties, with names like Chojuro, Kikusui, Nijesseiki, Doitsu, Imamura, are classified according to skin color. Skin may be brown or russet, yellowish brown or greenish brown, or yellowish green, often with a fine matte finish. The shape may be round (Japanese) or pear (Chinese).

Asian pears do not become melting ripe like Bartletts, but rather reach a sort of "*al dente*" or crisp-tender maturity. However you describe their texture, they should seethe with puddles of liquid like a juicy cucumber. And they should be as refreshing as a dip in an icy lake on a scorching day.

Asian pears can fit into any role the apple serves in cooked and uncooked preparations. They are good in salads with fruit or vegetables. They are a tasty and interesting variation on the theme of fruit pies, tarts, cobblers, and betty, where they retain their apple-fresh flavor. Cooked Asian pears keep their bitable texture, rather than liquidating into a puree. Steep them in liqueur or sprinkle them with brown sugar and cinnamon and bake like pears and apples.

You can find the different varieties of Asian pears from June through winter. Though its color will deepen, the fruit remains hard even when ripe. Store Asian pears in a cool, dry place. Refrigerated, they will keep from summer to spring, retaining their strident crispness.

Asian Pear Cheese Filling for Crêpes

 *4 to 6 servings*

1 cup water
½ cup brown sugar
½ teaspoon cinnamon
6 medium Asian pears, peeled, cored, and sliced
¼ cup golden raisins
⅔ cup ricotta cheese
¼ cup heavy cream
½ cup chopped walnuts
10 to 12 6-inch crêpes

1. In a large saucepan simmer water, sugar, cinnamon, pears, and raisins until pears are softened, about 25 minutes. Drain, reserving juice.

2. Combine ricotta, cream, and walnuts in a large bowl. Stir in slightly cooled pear mixture. Divide mixture among crêpes, folding each over to make a roll. Place crêpes in a chafing dish. Bring reserved juice to a boil and pour over crêpes. Serve immediately.

Variations: Use filling for pancakes, cakes, or as a breakfast spread for toast.

Breadfruit

Breadfruit, native to the Malay archipelago, is a high carbohydrate fruit popular in Guatemala, the Philippines, Indonesia, and Hawaii. The fruit, most often cooked in savory preparations as a vegetable would be, resembles a green wrinkled melon and is eaten at both unripe and ripe stages by natives in those countries. The yellow-green flesh is wrested from the crinkled green skin, sliced, and baked in a moderate oven for about 20 to 25 minutes until it is tender. Cooking brings forth the aroma of warmly baked bread with a chewy texture, which explains this fruit's name. The less ripe fruit has cool-mint-green skin and flesh and tastes drier and earthier than the ripened yellow fruit, which is sweeter and more yamlike.

Buy the fruit only in its firm stage, as soft fruit may be rotten. The green fruit may emit a white milky sap that does not affect quality. Store in a cool place and use within a few days. If you want the fruit ripe, leave it at room temperature until it is soft to the touch, sometimes with a brown speckled peel. Remove the peel and inner core before cooking. Slice or chunk the fruit before baking on a cookie sheet.

In countries where breadfruit is a starch staple it most often appears on the table as a potato, rice, or bread accompaniment would. Slices may also be fried into savory chips or the fruit may be boiled and simply seasoned, echoing our own potato passions. The sweeter mature soft fruit may be cooked and pureed into a dish resembling applesauce. Or it may be made into a chilled thick soup. Milk, sugar, and spices may also go into the cooked puree to yield a filling dessert high in energy-sustaining complex carbohydrates. Puddings, cakes, and pies can all be fashioned from the cooked ripe fruit.

Dilled Breadfruit Soup

 *4 to 6 servings*

3½ cups peeled, cored, and chunked breadfruit
2 tablespoons butter or vegetable oil
1 medium onion, chopped
2 stalks celery, chopped
1 carrot, chopped
3 cups chicken or vegetable stock
1½ cups light cream or milk
½ cup yogurt
3 tablespoons chopped fresh dill, or 2 tablespoons dried
Salt and pepper to taste
Watercress leaves

1. Place breadfruit in a saucepan, cover with water, and simmer until tender, about 35 to 40 minutes. Drain and allow breadfruit to cool when done.

2. Heat butter or oil in a skillet. Add onion, celery, and carrot and sauté over moderate heat for 10 minutes.

3. Puree breadfruit and cooked vegetables in a blender or food processor while adding stock slowly to mixture. If necessary, puree in batches and blend. Blend in cream, yogurt, dill, salt, and pepper. Chill and garnish each serving with watercress leaves.

Carambola (Star Fruit)

Its name sounds more like an island dance or percussive instrument than a fruit. Its appearance suggests a cubist's version of a banana or other curious objet d'art. Jane Grigson, author of *Jane Grigson's Fruit Book* (Atheneum, 1982), calls it an "amusing fruit." Five prominent ribs meander up its very thin and glossy yellow rind. Slicing crosswise transforms this funny fruit into perfect five-pointed stars or "starfish" (hence its common name, *star fruit*) that yield to all manner of use.

Its name derives from the Indian *kamrangea*, and indeed you will find a popular chutney that takes its tart aspects from star fruit. Native to Malaysia, the carambola now grows in good supply in Hawaii, South and Central America, and in the Caribbean. Chinese immigrants or sandalwood traders probably brought the tree to America years ago. Commercial Florida and California growers today produce enough star fruit to survive frequent bouts of cold weather. With its increasing popularity they have incentive to try harder. Early fall to midwinter is the peak season for this intriguing fruit.

Borne on a small tree, the fruit is 3 to 5 inches long and lobe-shaped. Its firm flesh is crisp and juicy with citrus highlights. My first taste of star fruit was as a palate-cleanser served during an informal wine tasting. Gently refreshing and unintrusive, the fruit worked well as unadorned taste teasers. In fact, its Indian name means "appetizer."

It is not necessary to peel away the shiny skin, but do wash star fruit, as you should all fruit. The fluted ribs may feature tough strings at their apex that you can easily pare away. While there are about twenty varieties, the sour-sweet Golden Star being the best known, this translucent yellow or yellow-green fruit usually has one of two distinct traits—sweet or sour. Both types are pleasant and both have equally worthy culinary applications. Coloring is the main key to which type you're buying. The richer the yellow of the shining skin, generally, the tarter the fruit. Although it may be sharp and acidic, the fruit won't be too harsh to eat raw—though it may warrant a sprinkle of sugar. Leaner ribs may also indicate a more sour variety.

Choose firm fruits with sturdy, fleshy ribs. Bruised or shriveled spots indicate poor quality. If the fruit's wings are green-tinged let it ripen at room temperature to full yellow. A flowery scent will indicate developed flavor. Store carambolas at room temperature for up to a couple of days. Refrigerate them if fully ripe, about seven to ten days.

Carambolas can garnish anything that lemon, lime, or orange slices do—punches and cocktails, seafood, poultry. Use them as a taste and textural contrast to smooth, creamy custards and puddings, or pies and cheesecakes. They are an easy way to improve fruit or vegetable salads and a clever way to flavor ices, mousses, and sherbets. Carambola slices retain a fresh-looking appearance and do not brown.

Sweet or sour star fruit may also appear in jam, jelly, pickles, or relish. You can sauté slices of star fruit quickly in butter with a sprinkle of fresh herb for a more interesting edible garnish or accompaniment to fish and chicken entrées. Cream cheese or other mild soft cheeses are an appealing foil for the tart, juicy fruit.

With noteworthy doses of vitamin C and potassium, star fruit is a perfectly healthy refresher after a hard run or other workout—why not as an elegant replacement for the traditional orange sections? The fruit is also low in calories, about 50 per 4-inch fruit.

Carambola Potpourri with Frangelico

 *6 to 8 servings*

This works well with either the sweet or the tart star fruit.

3 medium-size sweet carambolas, sliced
1 pound sweet cherries, pitted
1 pound seedless green grapes
½ pint blueberries
¼ cup shredded coconut
¼ cup Frangelico liqueur, or to taste

Combine all ingredients in a large bowl, preferably glass to show off the rainbow of colors. Serve chilled.

Cherimoya

A squat pinecone, a hand grenade, a barbless artichoke, armorlike reptile skin, leathery lizardlike hide—can all these descriptives refer to the appearance of anything of pleasurable taste? The tropics seem to be a haven for such incongruent edibles as the delicious cherimoya, an ancient fruit belonging to the Annonaceae family along with the soursop and sweetsop, or sugar apple. (Sometimes any one of them may be confusingly called custard apple—and, to confuse you even more, there is a hybrid called the atemoya [*Annona hybrid*], or Florida cherimoya, which is a cross between the cherimoya and the sweetsop.) Inside the cherimoya's swollen olive-green strawberry shape is a cream-colored pulp that is mildly musky with a suspicion of pineapple, banana, papaya, and strawberry.

The cool, dry slopes of the Andes are the birthplace of the custardlike fruit. The Incas, whose Quechua language named cherimoya for its "cold seeds," cultivated the wild tree from the Peruvian and Ecuadoran highlands. Mexico, Spain, the French Riviera, Florida, and California are now also home to the fruit. Although the coarse green skin with its bas-relief scallops looks tough as rawhide, the fruit does not travel well. Therefore, fruit to be shipped is picked at a fairly unripe, firm stage—so those of us removed from tropical climes cannot savor its natural tree-ripened essence. This fruit has a few cultivating, marketing, and shipping obstacles to overcome before it secures anything more than a sporadic niche in our markets' produce sections.

The cherimoya flesh is laced with slippery plump seeds like those of a watermelon. For use in recipes, you can sieve the soft pulp and leave the seeds behind.

Connoisseurs are fond of this delicate fruit in its pure unadorned state. Cut it into wedges and sharpen its mellow sweetness with a squirt of citrus—orange or lemon is nice, but lime is particularly recommended. The fruit's silken, somewhat grainy texture (like a smooth sherbet) can be enjoyed right out of the skin with a spoon, chilled or at room temperature. Simply slice off an opening at the top. Some fanciers of the fruit say a dash of cream or milk is an extravagant but delightful embellishment.

Add cherimoya chunks to fruit salads—berries, grapes, and other tropical fruits are fitting complements. The fruit's tender creamy flesh is a well-suited base to the ice cream family of desserts including parfaits, sorbets, and soufflés. It can be pureed alone or with other tangy fruit and lavished as a sauce upon ice cream, custards, pound or sponge cake. Use the sieved fruit in blended drinks with other fruit—bananas, raspberries, peaches—and in yogurt for a filling, healthy meal. Cherimoya contributes fiber, vitamin C, and the B-vitamin niacin. Add a dash of cinnamon and vanilla flavoring. Blended with orange juice and milk or cream, it becomes reminiscent of the luscious Creamsicles I enjoyed as a child.

Although this heart-shaped fruit may weigh up to 6 or 8 pounds, you are most likely to see fruit from 3 to 7 inches weighing ½ to 2 pounds. November to May is its peak season. Choose the largest fruit available to you. The cherimoya is fully green when it is ripe; look for a uniform color among its rows of stubby spines. Avoid cracked or darkly browned skin. You can let the fruit ripen at room temperature until it yields to gentle pressure, like an avocado. Do not let it overripen and do not chill unripe fruit. Once ripe, refrigerate and use within three to four days.

Cherimoya Almond Cream

 *6 servings*

1½ to 2 pounds very ripe cherimoya
1 pint heavy cream, whipped to firm peaks
3 tablespoons extrafine sugar
¼ teaspoon almond extract
¼ teaspoon nutmeg
⅓ cup plus 2 tablespoons slivered almonds, toasted

1. Scoop cherimoya flesh from shell, removing all seeds. Puree flesh in blender or food processor.

2. Fold cherimoya into whipped cream. Stir in sugar, almond extract, nutmeg, and ⅓ cup almonds.

3. Spoon mixture into 6 dessert ramekins. Distribute remaining almonds over top of each serving. Chill at least 2 hours before serving.

Feijoa

New Zealand, source of the once-exotic kiwi fruit, is also our current source of the feijoa (pronounced fay-JOE-ah or fay-YO-ah). This lime-green fruit has an elliptical egg or lemon shape and a perfumy fragrance. It blends wafts of citrus with menthol and pine forest. One whiff of this fruit transported me back to grammar school at Christmastime. Its scent is a duplicate of the hard candy the nuns gave us for the holiday, but its taste is far more refreshingly complex. In fact, I find it is a continuum of flavors that move around on your tongue. From the skin to the gelatinous center, the taste varies from slightly bitter and tangy to sweet and fruity, to that of eucalyptus-evergreen, and finally to something spiced with ginger, nutmeg, or cardamom. Some describe its taste as a cross between pineapple and banana, but I don't detect that at all.

The texture, varied also, is slightly granular, but smooth like a moist banana, now juicy, now jellylike. A cross section of the feijoa reveals a tan-yellow veined middle enclosed by a greenish outer perimeter. Although I find the skin edible, some find it unpleasantly bitter. It can be removed easily with a potato peeler or paring knife.

The subtropical fruit is native to southern Brazil, Paraguay, Uruguay, and northern Argentina, but our commercial supply arrives primarily from New Zealand during spring and early summer. California has begun to produce and distribute a fall crop. The feijoa is sometimes confused with the pineapple guava. The two fruits are related, but not the same. The feijoa is not a true guava, though its texture is reminiscent of the equally fragrant guava. The feijoa is an excellent source of vitamin C and contains less sugar than many other fruits.

A hard sniff will tell you a feijoa's worth. It should have a very pronounced bouquet of floral fruitiness. When ripe, it feels soft like a ripe tomato. Let firm fruit ripen at room temperature for a couple days, then refrigerate for up to three days. You can peel and puree the fruit for myriad cooking uses. The pureed fruit also freezes well in a tightly sealed container for up to six months.

With its mentholated scent, feijoa adds a pleasant and novel twist to fruit concoctions. Cut the fruit in half lengthwise and scoop out the soft pulp with a spoon for the quickest, most straight-forward treat. If you are unsure of its appeal to uninitiated diners, serve it sliced or wedged on a platter with other fruits, with a light dusting of sugar if its bitter note seems dominant.

The fruit can stand in as the flavoring agent in just about any dessert, including chilled ice and ice cream confections, pies, cobblers, and tarts, and fruit toppings and filling for cakes and custards. For a simple treatment, poach slices of the fruit in a light syrup and serve with a dollop of yogurt or crème fraîche. Add orange or lemon zest and nutmeg or ginger to the syrup to enliven the compote even more. You can even dab feijoa halves with butter and prepare them as you would baked pears or apples with wine and brown sugar or maple syrup and walnuts.

If you are fond of fruit-sweetened sauces for meat, game, or fowl consider adding feijoa's tang to them. Use the fruit either sliced or pureed.

Feijoa Maple Mousse

 *6 to 8 servings*

¼ cup sugar
½ cup water
1 pound ripe feijoas, peeled and sliced
4 eggs
½ cup maple syrup

1½ cups heavy cream, whipped to soft peaks
¼ cup finely chopped nuts (optional)

1. Simmer sugar, water, and feijoas in saucepan for 7 minutes. Set aside to cool.
2. In top of a double boiler, beat eggs lightly, and gradually add syrup. Set over hot water and cook until thick and smooth, about 10 minutes, stirring constantly. Remove from heat and cool.
3. Puree cooked feijoas in blender or food processor. Gently stir puree into egg mixture. Fold in whipped cream. Spoon into 6 or 8 parfait glasses. Chill for at least 4 hours. Top each parfait with chopped nuts just before serving.

Guava

The guava, its name deriving from the Spanish *guayaba*, thrives in the tropical and subtropical areas of the Americas and Asia. The crop is now grown in warm climates across the globe, including India, Cuba, Hawaii, and Florida, where most of those we purchase in the United States originate. As a fruit that flourishes with speed and abandon—it is considered a pest in some parts of the world—it appears in over one hundred varieties. We rarely see any fruit grown outside this country, unless it is first sprayed to protect it from the fruit fly (to which the fruit is highly susceptible).

The pale chartreuse- or olive-green-skinned guava is an imperfect oval or plum-round shape that is about 2 to 4 inches in diameter. The flesh ranges from white to peachy salmon and deeply crimson-blushed. Some varieties are spared the edible seeds, while others are packed with them. The seeds gravitate toward the center, with the outer flesh being grainy smooth like that of a pear. The fruit's Aztec name, *Xalxocotl*, meaning "sand plum," refers to this quality. Guavas are sweet, sometimes with a faint berrylike tartness.

The most alluringly salient aspect of the guava is its scent. Its heady perfume is said to dominate open-air tropical markets when it is in season. Indeed, cooking the fruit infuses a whole house with its seductive fragrance. The guava is kin to several other intensely aromatic plants in the myrtle family—eucalyptus, allspice, and cloves. In olden days, deep topaz-tinted guava jelly was quite popular, though it is much less so today. Guava juice and canned guava paste, a confection made by reducing strained guava pulp until very thick, are easily found in stores catering to a Spanish-speaking community.

Although the guava's rind is thick, it will give to gentle pressure when the fruit is ripe. Choose smooth-skinned, unblemished guavas that have a somewhat pronounced floral scent. Those that are firm, on the verge of ripening, are the best. Let ripen at room temperature for a day or so. Use ripe guavas within two days, as they quickly turn dry and woolly.

Guavas provide you with more vitamin C than many citrus fruits—about 240 milligrams per 3½-ounce serving—several times over the recommended daily allowance. They are also a good source of vitamin A and potassium. Enjoy the guava raw if you like. Quarter the fruit and remove the seeds with a knife or grapefruit spoon or chop and add guava to fruit salads.

Guava compote is a favorite Mexican sweet. It can enhance a fruit relish. The fruit also successfully lends its taste and aroma to ice cream and hot and cold soufflés. Pureed guava can be made into mousse, pudding, or blender drinks and also makes a simple but excellent sauce for roast pork or poultry.

Guava Compote

 *4 servings*

10 ripe guavas
½ cup honey
1 cup orange juice
1 tablespoon fresh lemon juice
1 cinnamon stick

Wash but do not peel guavas. Quarter and remove seeds with spoon or tip of knife. Combine honey, orange juice, lemon juice, and cinnamon stick in a large heavy saucepan. Bring to a boil and add guava wedges. Simmer over low heat for about 10 minutes, taking care not to overcook or guavas will disintegrate. Allow compote to cool. Serve over plain cake or ice cream, or by itself with whipped cream or yogurt.

Kiwi Fruit

The kiwi fruit is native to China, where it is called *Yang tao*, but the fruit does not figure on even a small scale in Chinese cuisine. Introduced to New Zealand at the turn of the century as the Chinese gooseberry, it is a woody vine that grows up to 30 feet long, entwining any available support. The kiwi fruit (renamed such after the New Zealand bird when it was marketed in this country) can grow in southern, western, and southeastern border states here. It is grown commercially in California during New Zealand's off-season and so is available to us year round.

The fruit is an oval berry the size and shape of an egg and grows on the vine in grapelike clusters. Happily, the skin is resilient enough to protect the fruit during long-distance travel. Its thick honey-brown skin is fuzzy or suedelike and it encases the most exquisite jewel-green flesh. Shining black onyx seeds radiate out from a light yellow center, forming a perfect ebony sun design in the translucent emerald flesh. The tiny seeds are edible and barely perceptible when eaten.

The firm melonlike flesh is sweet and slurpy with hints of lime, strawberry, melon, and a citrus freshness. Kiwis are a featured element in a famous dessert, the Pavlova, that comes from down under. It is a pudding conceived for Anna Pavlova when she visited Australia in the 1930s. It consists of a meringue, passion fruit, cream, and kiwi fruit, a veritably rich and aristocratic concoction.

Buy kiwis when they are fairly plump and firm, more like ripe peaches than ripe plums, which are too mushy. The fruit should give slightly when squeezed in the palm of your hand. Ripen it in a paper bag at room temperature for a couple days. You can refrigerate unripe fruit and then ripen as desired. You can slice fully ripe fruit and freeze for up to six months. Sweetness may diminish slightly, but texture will not suffer.

Kiwi fruit is extremely versatile. Its acid-sweetness balance makes it good for blending with mild-flavored fruits. The furry skin peels away quite easily. Kiwi is a pleasurable treat eaten out of hand, chilled or not. Simply cut in half lengthwise and scoop out the fruit with a spoon. Kiwis have twice the vitamin C of oranges.

It is best not to crowd the kiwi fruit's spectacular elegance with too many kinds of fruits in a salad. Mix it with two or three others of contrasting color and texture. Or simply slice it with other attractive fruits, such as carambola, guava, and mango.

Kiwi is also a colorful garnish that glitters atop many dishes. Like papaya's papsain enzyme, kiwi contains a meat-tenderizing element that also keeps gelatin from setting. Blanching the kiwi slightly (and carefully, as it is very delicate) will deactivate this quality, if you want to add it to gelatin. Add circles of kiwi to cole slaw, to potato, chicken, and turkey salads, or to fruit punches and cocktails. Top cereal with kiwi slices and cream. Serve kiwi with mild-tasting avocado slices. The jade fruit makes a plain white cheesecake look absolutely stunning; with an added glaze, it is an eye-catching centerpiece. Garnish poultry and meat dishes with kiwi cartwheels.

Shrimp and Kiwi Appetizer

 *4 servings*

2 tablespoons butter or vegetable oil
3 medium kiwis, peeled and sliced
1 pound small shrimp, cooked and shelled
2 teaspoons fresh lemon juice
Salt and freshly ground black pepper to taste
1 tablespoon chopped fresh Italian parsley

1. Heat butter or oil in skillet. Add kiwi slices and shrimp and sauté just until heated through, about 2 minutes.
2. Add lemon juice and salt and pepper to taste. Place shrimp and kiwi in serving dish and garnish with parsley.

Kumquats

Golden-orange kumquats have long made an attractive splash amid the green produce at Chinatown markets. About the size of robins' eggs, they look like miniature oranges (their Cantonese name means "miniature orange"). The round or oval-shaped fruit is a common sight on lacquered trays in the Orient, where it appears as ornamental food. Festive kumquats grow on fine-stemmed and bushy evergreen shrubs that also serve a popular decorative function on terraces, patios, and in gift packaging.

Kumquats are like oranges turned inside out—they have a sweet spicy rind that is thin and edible and their interior pulp is tart, a pleasant blend of tastes. Kumquats were once classified as a citrus fruit, but botanists reconsidered a while back and gave the kumquat its own genus, *Fortunella*. The golden nuggets are closely related to the citruslike calamondin and to mandarin oranges. The cold-resistant fruit thrives in Florida and California. Botanists have also developed a whole line of "cross-quats"—limequats, orangequats, and citrangequats—but none of these is widely grown. *Nagami* is the name of the kumquat variety commonly grown in this country.

The crisp sweetness of these palm-size oranges is easily enjoyed. Loaded with vitamin C, potassium, and some vitamin A and calcium, they make an exotic breakfast treat or out-of-hand snack. Their sunny brightness and petit-four demeanor enliven hors d'oeuvres trays and they make a pretty, edible garnish when sliced, quartered, or wedged. They add a bold acid-sweet burst of flavor to mixed greens. Halve them and combine with other colorful fruit—cherries, grapes, blueberries, kiwi, melon balls—for a kaleidoscopic presentation. They contain some seeds, which you can easily flick out with a knife.

Kumquats take well to a variety of preparations, too. Halve and stuff them with cream cheese. Simmered in a syrup, they release their citrus zest and retain their firmness. Use them in any meat or game sauces that use oranges. They can be pureed and used to flavor baked goods, frostings, and filling creams. Kumquats are also a popular preserve, jam, or marmalade base.

The fruit is available from December to May, with its peak season in early winter. Look for firm, bright, and glossy fruit that are heavy for their size. Squeeze gently to determine ripeness. Ripe fruit will host mold if left too long at warm room temperature. Kumquats spoil more quickly than thicker-skinned oranges, but will keep for up to a month in the refrigerator. Wash before eating to remove fungicides.

Golden Kumquats and Greens
with Walnut Dressing

 *4 servings*

½ cup walnut oil
¼ cup raspberry vinegar
¼ teaspoon salt, or to taste
⅛ teaspoon white pepper
1 clove garlic, halved
1 small head of arugula, trimmed, washed, and dried
½ small head red-leaf lettuce, cleaned and torn into small
   pieces
1 bunch watercress
4 thin slices large red onion, separated into rings
8 kumquats, thinly sliced and seeded

1. Combine oil, vinegar, salt, and pepper in a small pitcher and stir gently.
2. Rub large salad bowl with garlic halves. Toss greens in with onion rings and kumquats. Pour dressing over greens and toss to coat well. Divide salad onto 4 salad platters and serve.

Litchi

The litchi has a legendary romantic niche in the minds of the Chinese. It is associated with one of their emperors, who went to great lengths to satisfy his concubine's capricious desire for the sensuous fruit—sensuous, that is, once freed of its scruffy, embossed jacket. Amorous attachments aside, the Chinese sport a genuine affinity for the sweet, juicy, and intriguing fruit. It has long appeared in their marketplace and their cuisine. And it may take great lengths to obtain the fruit, for it grows in clusters on tall evergreen trees reaching 40 feet. What's more, the tree takes its time maturing, and may dawdle a good ten to twelve years before it shows fruit.

The coveted flesh of the fruit is silver-white and translucent, firm and lightly veined. It resembles a peeled grape and is smooth and elegant. Even its leathery shell, or pericarp, with its russet or cherry-rose coloring, is attractive—a perfect still-life subject for a watercolor artist.

A dark-brown central pit, smooth as olive wood, is embedded in the walnut-size fruit, or aril. Flesh, shell, and seed are easily separated. The grapelike pulp is pleasantly chewy and lightly violet-scented, reminiscent of jasmine. For a first encounter try adding litchi's elegance to a simple fruit cup or atop ice cream. Serve the pearly globes as a wine and cocktail accompaniment. Suspend them diaphanously in gelatin molds, or bejewel a fresh summer fruit tart with litchis, along with grapes, purple plum halves, and scarlet berries.

The litchi has only a short season, from early June to early July. It can be stored for several weeks, preferably in the refrigerator, or frozen in the jacket for a few months. The fruit's firmness will diminish, but taste will remain fairly intact. Select full litchis that feel heavy for their size and have no damaged or shriveled shells. Browning is perfectly acceptable and a maraschino-cherry color indicates freshness.

Mediterranean Trout and Litchis

 *4 to 6 servings*

5 peppercorns
2 bay leaves
½ small onion, unpeeled
1 sprig parsley
½ carrot, unpeeled
½ stalk celery
½ lemon
2 cups water
2 pounds (about 3) whole trout

Dressing
⅔ cup virgin olive oil
½ teaspoon grated fresh ginger
Juice of 1 large lemon
1 clove garlic, minced
2 teaspoons dried oregano, crumbled
¼ teaspoon salt
¼ teaspoon crushed red pepper
10 litchis, shelled and pitted

1. Combine peppercorns, bay leaves, onion, parsley, carrot, celery, lemon, and water in a large saucepan. Bring to a boil, add trout, and gently simmer until fish becomes opaque and flakes easily with a fork, about 5 minutes. Allow fish to cool in poaching liquid.

2. Combine oil, ginger, lemon juice, garlic, oregano, salt, and red pepper in a large bowl.

3. When fish is cool, remove skin and bones and flake flesh into a bowl with dressing. Halve litchis and add to bowl. Toss

gently to coat well. Marinate in refrigerator for at least 4 hours. Serve as appetizer or lunch entrée.

Mango

What do the cashew, the pistachio, and poison ivy have in common? They're all relatives of the tropical mango fruit, in the family Anacardiaceae. Yet none of its siblings can match its blazing appearance. Piles of ripening mangoes are a warming sight at fruit stands more and more often as this luscious fruit emerges from oblivion in our temperate zones. Its brilliant rainbow of reds, yellows, oranges, and greens radiates an irresistible glow. In the bustling dinginess of New York City streets I have taken visual solace from the bright fruit piled high in the Korean grocers' bins.

Florida, California, and Hawaii produce the fruit available in this country. Mangoes grow on a dome-canopied evergreen that can reach between 30 and 130 feet tall and live for over a century. The fruit varies from 1 to 12 inches long, ranging in weight from several ounces to over 5 pounds, and in shape from round to ovoid-oblong. Borne on a small tree, the fruit is 3 to 5 inches long. The skin is thick and smooth as kid leather and the flesh is a dazzling Crayola yellow to orange, with a dense silken texture like that of no other fruit. It combines the firmness of fresh sushi and the meltingness of a creamy custard. It has a cleansing juiciness with citrus overtones and many notes on the tropical scale.

Aroma and flavor are its star attributes. Its peachy sweetness, modified by an ineffable musky essence, is sometimes redolent of syrupy liqueurs. Think peach brandy, Amaretto, or Frangelico. In fact, mangoes soaked in one of the three would be heavenly. Mangoes suspended in a hearty red wine are even more divine— a ruby-golden ambrosial treat.

The only minor drawback to mangoes is the center stone that clings tenaciously to the buttery fruit. More annoying than its steadfast hold is the stone's indefinable shape. You need to dislodge a few (and sacrifice some clods of your treasured nectar) before you are quite sure where its limits extend in the soft juicy flesh. You can peel the fruit easily enough with a potato peeler or paring knife, then slice it down and across the flat ridged stone.

Florida mangoes are in peak season throughout the summer, and some imported varieties may appear from January through the fall months. Select underripe fruit that is green and slightly blushed with rose, peach, or yellow tones. The skin should be taut and smooth like a well-developed muscle, never pitted or dimpled with a cellulite finish. The fruit ripens at room temperature in a few days and is best kept in a brown bag. Ready-to-eat ripe mangoes become streaked with brighter color (unless they are the green mango variety) and yield to slight pressure like avocados. Sniff the fruit too for some perfume and pass it by if it hints of turpentine. Refrigerate as soon as ripe and keep for up to a week. You can puree the peeled succulent pulp and freeze it for several months.

Mango on its own is the simplest of elegant treats. Mango slices with yogurt are a fine healthy snack, the fruit giving you a good dose of vitamins A and C and potassium. Mangoes and cream, mangoes on shortcake, on rice pudding, on granola, in chicken salad—the fruit is infinitely versatile.

The golden flesh translates into the finest desserts, too: ice cream and ices, mousse, pies, tarts, upside-down cakes, crumb-topped cobblers. Mangoes, especially the acid-sweet green ones, seem to have an established niche in relishes, pickles, and chutneys, all of which pair famously with meat, game, and poultry. I have found curried mango chutney to be of well-balanced spice and tang, great with a roasted chicken. Many salads and vegetable dishes are improved by the addition of mango slices, chunks, or wedges. The firm pulp stands up well to cooking and makes a deliciously balmy dessert or savory sauce.

Sweet-and-Sour Mango Chutney

 *4 to 6 servings*

2 to 3 (about 2 pounds) large ripe mangoes
2 tablespoons peanut oil
1 small onion, minced
1 tablespoon sugar
1 tablespoon cider vinegar
2 teaspoons lemon juice
¼ teaspoon cinnamon
⅛ teaspoon each of cardamom, ground cloves, cumin, nutmeg,
   ground ginger, and cayenne pepper

1. Peel mangoes and separate pulp from stone over bowl to catch juice. Mash pulp with potato masher or wooden spoon.
2. Heat oil in large skillet. Add onion and cook until soft, about 5 minutes. Stir in mango and remaining ingredients. Cook and stir about 5 minutes longer. Serve hot with roasted chicken or meat. Serve plain yogurt alongside the chutney for a pleasant contrast in flavors.

Papaya

Under broad spiraling foliage grow clusters of suggestively shaped papayas (the name derives from the Carib *ababal*). In her book *Uncommon Fruits and Vegetables* (Harper & Row, 1986), Elizabeth Schneider refers to the fruit as the tree's "mammary-like burdens." The misshapen fruit indeed easily resembles a lumpy Rodin sculpting of voluptuous breasts. The plant can be either male, female, or hermaphroditic. Male plants do not reproduce, and the extremely fertile females require the presence of a male. As for the hermaphrodites, they're self-pollinating.

The trees that bear fruit do so early in life and generously. The only problem once besetting the prolific plant was fruit size, which could unpredictably reach well over 10 pounds. Happily now, scientific intervention has given us the down-sized Solo, weighing ½ to 2 pounds (actually a two- to three-person serving). Most of our papayas come from Hawaii, and are available year round, with peaks in summer and spring.

The thin, rindlike skin ranges in color from cool melon green to rose-flushed or buttery yellow. The interior flesh is soft, silky, and dense like that of the mango, though its flavor is a blushing violet compared to that assertive fruit. Papaya is more mild and subtle like a melon (it is sometimes referred to as a "tree melon"), lacking any acid notes. A good ripe one is sweet, pulpy, and refreshing.

Papaya's womblike hollow is packed with charcoal-gray seeds, shining and incandescent like the caviar spawn of beluga. The seeds are edible and have sharp, peppery notes that are good crushed in vinaigrette dressings or used whole and glistening as a garnish upon sunny crescents of papaya.

When ripe, papaya will be awash in sunny yellow. Its ripe state feels like that of an avocado or a kiwi—gently giving but not mushy. Partly ripe fruit will develop in a warm kitchen. Chill when ripe and serve within a couple of days. Flaws and spots in the skin do not hurt the flesh's quality, provided the feel and coloring are right.

This shy fruit is good in salads and fruit cups, but needs to be coaxed out of oblivion with more acid ingredients. I first savored papaya in a Mazatlán youth hostel as part of a mouth-watering mélange with pineapple and coconut atop steaming pancakes. Meat, poultry, or vegetable salads can effectively elevate its fragile texture and subdued flavor to savory heights. A spritz of fresh lime juice wakes up its sleepy flavor, if you care to eat the fruit simply.

Cubed as a tropical tidbit, or skewered with meat, shellfish, or vegetables, papaya can take a grilling. Turn the halved fruit into an edible ice cream dish, a shrimp boat, or a salad bowl. You can stuff and bake the fruit as you would squash. In fact, the green fruit, which must be cooked, often doubles as a vegetable.

You can parlay satiny papaya pulp into all manner of desserts, especially creamy soft ones, including custards, puddings, and sweet sauces. Like banana, the pulp is easily mashed or pureed. Give the American baked-fruit favorites—buckle, pandowdy, cobbler, grunt, and shortcake—an exotic base with papaya. Poach the fruit in a light syrup, enhancing its flavor with spices such as ginger, mace, cinnamon, nutmeg, and cardamom, or with orange zest.

What it lacks in acid, papaya makes up for in enzyme. Papain, found in the latex of the juice, bark, and leaves of the papaya tree, has long been used to tenderize meat. The enzyme (which is not in the ripe fruit) is also a famous digestive aid.

Curried Papaya and Chicken Salad

 *4 to 6 servings*

½ cup mayonnaise
½ cup plain yogurt
1½ tablespoons whole grain mustard
¼ cup minced celery
¼ cup minced green pepper
1 tablespoon minced onion
1 tablespoon curry powder
1 teaspoon sugar
¼ teaspoon black pepper
1 large ripe papaya, peeled and halved
1 tablespoon reserved papaya seeds
2 pounds cooked chicken breast, cut into 1-inch pieces
5 or 6 washed, dried firm lettuce leaves
2 tablespoons chopped fresh tarragon or parsley

1. Combine mayonnaise, yogurt, mustard, celery, green pepper, onion, curry powder, sugar, and black pepper in a large bowl. Mix well.

2. Cut papaya into slices, about ½ inch by 1½ inches. Crush seeds with a mortar and pestle, a garlic press, or by pressing them on a cutting board with a large knife handle. Add papaya, seeds, and chicken to dressing and toss gently to coat well.

3. Spread lettuce leaves over a serving platter and turn salad onto leaves. Garnish with tarragon or parsley. Serve chilled.

Passion Fruit

The appearance of the passion fruit belies its name. About the size of a billiard ball, it is a dullish eggplant-purple color with a dimpled cardboardlike shell that is round or oval. The name emanates from the plant's flowers, which so impressed the pantheistic-minded Jesuit missionaries in South America, the fruit's native land. These Spanish clergy saw signs of Christ's passion in nature's artwork. Limned within parts of the beautiful bloom are the Three Nails, the Five Wounds, the Crown of Thorns, and the Apostles. In fitting accord with the fathers' vision, the flowers of the purple passion open at dawn and close at noon.

What biblical symbolism can there be in the heavenly scented and flavored nectar? Inside the mundane rind is the most highly coveted juice (available frozen for a proverbial arm and a leg). This paradisiacal essence is liquid-jelly-textured, chartreuse-tinted, and a conglomerate of lemony, honeysuckle, exotically spiced flavors. Packing, travel, and even processing cannot dissipate its intense quality. The only discouragement to some at first are the many slippery seeds swimming in the ambrosia. But the seeds are easily forgotten once you realize they are, like tomato seeds, edible and almost tasteless.

There is a yellow form of passion fruit that may have mutated from the purple form. It is called *yellow granadilla* (meaning "little pomegranate" in Spanish) and it is a golden color when ripe. You will most likely see only the purple passion fruit, the better tasting of the two, in our markets.

You can eat the drinkable pulp fresh from the sliced-open shell or rub it through a sieve to remove the seeds. The juice is a popular flavoring for chilled drinks, cake frostings, ice cream, sorbets, and mousses. The versatile fruit can be the basis for a seductive lemon curd or can work magic in jams, jellies, and many a condiment, including barbecue sauce. The rind is a good source of pectin, the jelly-firming substance.

It's easy enough to choose good fruit. They go from smooth to dimpled as they ripen. The larger and heavier the fruit, the better. The shell, like a favorite old suitcase, remains durable protection for its contents. Chill the ripe fruit for up to a week. Passion fruit is an excellent source of vitamins A and C.

Passion Fruit Sauce

 *Makes about 1¼ cups*

5 passion fruit
¼ cup water
½ cup white grape juice
2 tablespoons sugar
1 tablespoon cornstarch
¼ teaspoon grated lemon zest
¼ teaspoon cinnamon
3 tablespoons unsalted butter

1. Scoop pulp from passion fruit and sieve thoroughly to extract as much juice as possible from seeds. Discard seeds.

2. Combine water, juice, sugar, and cornstarch in a saucepan and bring to a boil slowly, then lower to a simmer. Add passion fruit juice, zest, cinnamon, and butter. Stir until butter melts. Serve hot over pancakes, crêpes, sponge cake, custard, or other dessert.

Variation: Add 2 tablespoons grated coconut or chopped nuts to sauce while hot.

Pepino

Once upon a time there were just two kinds of melon, honeydew and cantaloupe, available in the produce section of your local market. Then along came casaba, cranshaw, musk, Oriental, and Spanish melons, and a rainbow host of others, with flesh ranging from mint green to rosy peach, eggshell, and pearly white. The generic has gone out of the melon family. Presently, melon types seem to make only cameo appearances in the marketplace, here today, not to be seen again for a long time.

The pepino is yet another rising star in the melon cast, though it integrates characteristics of other fruits, namely pears and squash. And it may be more than a flash in the pan if California producers have their way. Its celebrity is already more than passing in Japan, where its chic appearance makes the highly esteemed fruit worthy as a gift. The pepinos in the United States come from New Zealand growers.

Its shape is evocative of a large acorn, a skewed heart, or a giant teardrop. Its skin, smooth as varnished oak, is yellow-gold, streaked with Easter-egg lavender.

Also called a *melon pear*, the pepino is like a melon in many ways, but with a tighter-weaved texture and seething with more juice. It is subtly sweet with an emphatic flowery quality, mildly like orange-blossom honey.

Look for the glossy-skinned fruit in late winter through early spring. The size may vary greatly—from about 2 to 6 inches in girth—but doesn't affect quality. Do be fussy about cosmetic appearance with this fruit, as it is a reliable indicator of the inner flesh's quality. The color should be brightly yellowed and pink, not dull or haggard. The skin should give to slight pressure when ripe. Store in the refrigerator and serve chilled.

Like other melon, the pepino is refreshing straight from its shell, though its mild flavor may be encouraged by a twist of lemon or lime. Like melon, it is no less an effective foil to cappacola, prosciutto, or other salty Italian hams.

Its central cavity is filled with edible seeds, which you can remove to make room (in the larger specimens) for ice cream or other chopped fruit and yogurt. You can blend the low-calorie, vitamin-A- and -C-rich pulp with other, tarter, sweeter fruits for a thirst-slaking beverage.

Pepino Antipasto

 6 *servings*

¼ cup extra virgin olive oil

2 tablespoons red wine vinegar

¼ teaspoon crushed red pepper

⅛ teaspoon sugar

12 ounces mozzarella (unsalted, if available), cut into 1-inch cubes

2 roasted sweet red peppers (seeded), coarsely chopped

10 Italian black olives

10 to 12 thin slices prosciutto

2 medium-size pepinos, cut into thin slices

Mix together oil, vinegar, crushed pepper, and sugar in a bowl. Toss in cheese, roasted peppers, and olives, and mix until well coated. Roll prosciutto slices into cylinders and arrange with pepino slices on a platter, in pinwheel fashion. Place cheese mixture in center of platter and serve with crusty Italian bread.

Persimmon

The appearance of the persimmon (mainly from a tropical tree) in a temperate climate "is a sort of horticultural accident," according to Rodale's *The Organic Gardener's Complete Guide to Vegetables and Fruits* (1982). Although this small, astringent American version (*Diospyros virginiana*) has no commercial impact today, it was one of the first fruits revered by early explorers. There is also the more common Japanese persimmon, called *kaki*, about 3 inches in diameter. The American name is from the Algonquin *putchamin* or *pessemin*. Today, California grows the Oriental variety available to us.

The squat bell-shaped fruit makes a stunning appearance with its peppermint-green stem collar atop its fiery orange body. When unripe the persimmon, like a tomato, is streaked with gold, the shades of a desert sky at sunset. When fully ripe its orange-scarlet is as vibrant and evocative as that of Gauguin's Tahitian paintings.

The delicate persimmon is well-known for its mouth-puckering tartness when eaten before its time. The astringency, due to its tannic acid (the bitter taste in black tea), will fade as the fruit ripens. Look for peak fruit from November through early March. Use the same selection guidelines as you would for tomatoes— choose firm, heavy fruit with sprightly coloring that promises to deepen and minimal blemishing. Place unripe fruit in a bag in the kitchen to ripen (an apple or banana in the same bag will encourage sweetness).

The persimmon feels smooth and tough-skinned when not fully developed, then becomes very soft and sloshy, and fragile—like vine-ripened Jersey tomatoes. When its transparent skin feels like a water balloon bursting with its contents, you may regale yourself with a wholesome vitamin-A-enriched treat. There may be no seeds or as many as ten. Store the ripe fruit in a cool place for a couple of days, or freeze it for several months.

When ripe, the persimmon's flesh is sweet and mellow, reminiscent of plums but dewy like apricots, with a pudding texture. Many cooks recommend simply piercing the skin of the elegant fruit and spooning out the flesh, with or without some cream as an enhancement. Freezing, then partially thawing the fruit, can yield a sherbetlike confection that can be eaten the same way.

Persimmons can also be mashed or pulped and incorporated into puddings, pies, and tartlets, and they lend a very deliciously pretty color to ice cream. Jane Grigson laments the "baked and sodden" treatments such as stewed puddings that American cookery has bestowed upon persimmons. But I think that what to her is the "heavy sadness" of these dishes is perhaps a dyed-in-the-wool American affinity for comfort food. (If you were raised on mashed potatoes and gravy, hotcakes and syrup, you'll know what I mean.)

You can serve glowing persimmon slices in salads, with other fruits, with meat or poultry, on canapés with cream cheese, or in fancier desserts from mousse and Bavarian creams to custard or cake filling. Lemon juice nudges its mellow taste to life, as do light touches of cinnamon, ginger, or nutmeg. Too much spicing will render it an anonymous entity. The Japanese forego their customary restraint and sprinkle the fruit lightly with sake. Try it, substituting tequila or a liqueur, for a light but potent dessert.

Persimmon Pudding

 *6 servings*

1½ cups persimmon puree
2 eggs
¾ cup heavy cream
1 teaspoon vanilla extract
2 tablespoons brandy
½ cup light brown sugar
½ cup unbleached flour
1½ teaspoons baking soda
¼ teaspoon cinnamon
¼ teaspoon nutmeg
⅛ teaspoon ground ginger
Crème fraîche or whipped cream

1. Preheat oven to 350° F. Beat together persimmon puree, eggs, cream, vanilla, brandy, and sugar until blended well.
2. Sift together flour, baking soda, cinnamon, nutmeg, and ginger. Add dry ingredients to wet and mix just until blended. Pour into lightly greased 2-quart baking dish. Bake for 35 to 40 minutes, until an inserted cake tester comes out clean. Serve warm with crème fraîche or whipped cream.

Plantain

Most people know that plantains are some exotic form of the bananas we eat in this country, but the curiosity ends there. The plantain would seem less exotic if more people were to see this tropical fruit outside its thick reddish or greenish coat. Much of its difference from the yellow banana is just skin deep. In fact, bananas and plantains are closely related ancient fruits, native to tropical Asia, and, oddly enough, are classified as herbs because they lack woody tissue in their stems.

The prevailing impression of plantains is that they are too gummy and starchy to eat raw and unadorned. But plantains are like the bananas we know and love: some are edible uncooked and some may never develop past a mushy blandness that is best for baking. Plantains are usually firmer than our familiar bananas, which makes them better suited to the popular fried preparation banana chips, often to be found in natural foods stores.

In some tropical climes the plantain is both an important commercial fruit and a homegrown staple for subsistence-level farmers. In Indian cuisine the plantain may appear curried in its skin, while fat red ones are offerings in Hindu ceremonies.

The plantain's cross-cultural heritage has established its reputation as a good cooking fruit. Yet in South American dishes the plantain is most often treated as a vegetable. Like our potatoes, it is considered an important source of dietary starch.

The plantains imported into this country are either the short, fat red kind or the long, thicker-skinned greenish ones with natural brown spots and rough patches on the skin. Once ripened, plantains are highly perishable. So, unless you intend to use it immediately, buy this fruit in a semiripe state. You can peel and freeze chunks of overly ripe fruit, storing them in plastic bags for cooking later. Store plantains as you would bananas, at room temperature. Refrigeration will turn them black.

Plantains are good baked or boiled and seasoned like white potatoes, prepared like candied sweet potatoes, or pureed and served with meat or poultry dishes. Cook this fruit either before it reaches ripeness (usually as a vegetable) or when very ripe (usually in sweet preparations).

Sautéed Plantain

This recipe is a very popular, delectable, and easy way to prepare this tropical fruit. The chips make a tasty confection or original accompaniment to a brunch menu.

Large, medium-ripe (firm) plantains
Butter or oil
Cinnamon and sugar

Slice the plantains lengthwise when still firm and just ripe into ½-inch thick pieces. Sauté the slices in a little butter or oil until golden brown. Dust with cinnamon and sugar. Serve hot.

℘omegranate (Chinese Apple)

I associate pomegranates (and Bing cherries and fresh strawberries) with a few opulent summers when my family of many siblings could afford such high-priced fruit. We called them Chinese apples and stained many a shirt and blouse with dribbles and squirts of the reddish-pink juice. It surprised me to discover that many of my peers had never even heard of the exotically constructed fruit.

The pomegranate is classified as a leathery berry (a rather large one, at 2½ to 5 inches in diameter) and grows on a bushy shrub that reaches up to 20 feet. The name, derived from Latin *pomum granatum*, means apple or fruit of seeds.

The thick rind, hard with a matte finish of rose to deep burgundy, is actually protection for the many seeds, the real spoils of the fruit. A juicy red pulp encases each seed, all lodged in a series of chambers, which are situated not unlike those of the human heart. The highly prized seeds packed in their compartments resemble a cathedral's stained-glass window design or miniature morsels of fine Venetian glass.

Eating this glamorous fruit involves a string of exceptional sensory stimuli. After ripping aside the astringent manila pith, you take in a mouthful of the easily dislodged rubies. You crush and suck them against the roof of your mouth—no teeth, yet—and ravish the full-bodied sweet-tart pulp and liquor that slithers freely down your gullet. Then you must decide whether to expectorate the spent seeds or, if you are not averse to their slight crunch, chew and swallow all. Both eating methods are equally respectable.

Look for pomegranates in the fall and early winter. Select brightly colored large fruits that are heavy for their size, like grapefruits. Look for a hard unbroken rind, avoiding those showing decay. Make sure the stem crown is not dry. The skin should be tough but malleable enough to reveal the imprint of the tightly crowded seeds inside. You can store the fruit for weeks at room temperature and for quite a long time if you refrigerate it—up to three months. The sturdy fruit improves with age, its sweet-wine pungency getting fuller and more pronounced. The skin color darkens to deep wine and the seeds soften and become more chewable.

If the pomegranate juice is the only object of your affection in this tactile fruit, extract it by squeezing the kernels in a cloth bag or with an orange press. The juice, the foundation of grenadine syrup, adds indescribable depth to drinks and punch bowls. Its acid notes round out savory sauces or add bite to dessert frostings or cold dessert soups. Pomegranate jelly is an unusual but delicious application.

I have seen pomegranate seeds bumping about mixed fruit salads—an attractive but futile addition, I feel. Pomegranates are a fine dessert fruit, but are too eccentric to blend with the mass of fruits. While the seeds are an integral part of the pomegranate experience, they may detract from the eating pleasure of other fruits.

You may try a sprinkling of the glassy seeds as glistening garnish on hot or cold meat or vegetable platters.

The Chinese apple is of nutritional interest to those who participate in any of today's fashionable endurance exercises, such as running, swimming, cycling, and aerobics. Phenomenally high in potassium, the juice will help replenish this depleted electrolyte after exhaustive workouts. The juice also supplies the all-around healthful vitamin C.

Pomegranate Sunrise

 *4 servings*

Here's a deliciously refreshing way to replenish those minerals and vitamins we exhaust daily.

2½ cups pomegranate seeds
½ cup sugar
3 to 4 cups freshly squeezed orange juice
4 cherries
4 lime slices

1. Place seeds in a saucepan and crush until juice escapes. Add sugar and simmer for about 5 minutes. Strain juice to remove all seeds. Allow juice to cool, then store in a glass jar and chill thoroughly.

2. Pour 1½ to 2 inches of pomegranate juice into bottom of 4 tall cocktail glasses. Fill glasses to top with orange juice. Garnish each with a cherry and a lime slice joined with a toothpick.

POMEGRANATE TEQUILA SUNRISE: Leave room for a shot of tequila to fill each glass.

POMEGRANATE SUNRISE MIMOSA: Leave room for ½ cup champagne to fill each glass.

Pomelo (Pummelo)

Just one look reveals that the pomelo is a member of the citrus family, the largest one, a sort of grapefruit in the rough. Called the grandfather of the latter, it sports the same textured rind and a lot thicker pith, the same tough membrane encasing fleshy juice vesicles. But it can be two to three times the size of the grapefruit, and it may be pear-shaped or round, with colors ranging from cream to pale yellow or pink.

The pomelo originated in China and made its debut in the New World in the seventeenth century through the grace of East Indian Captain Shaddock in the Barbados Islands. Called *chadec* in French, a corruption of the voyager's name, the pomelo was prized highly among the edible gifts of Eastern cultures and by European spice traders. Today the fruit grows in our Florida Keys and Everglades.

The pulp is sweet and with less juice, acidity, and bitterness than that of the grapefruit. Seed content varies with variety from almost seedless to a seed jungle. Judge good pomelos (available in winter) as you would grapefruit. They should be firm, heavy, with no soft or pitted patches that indicate either rot or dryness, and with plenty of citrus aroma. The fruit stores as well as grapefruit, too, at room temperature or chilled. Like other citrus fruits, pomelos contribute a good yield of vitamin C and potassium and are low in calories.

You can use pomelo as you would grapefruit—simply eaten fresh, baked with a sweet glaze, and thanks to its enormous pith, conserved like a marmalade. To prepare pomelo for fresh eating or for any use, extricate the pulp from the rind and pith, as well as from the durable membrane. Halve the sections and add them to fruit salads or serve as the sole ingredient of a fruit cup with honey or a sugar syrup and fresh lemon or lime juice. The fruit's pulpy pink or yellow flesh is a nice contrast for creamy-fleshed green avocado, making the following recipe not only savory but pretty.

Pomelo and Avocado Salad

 *4 to 6 servings*

2 pomelos
1 ripe avocado, peeled and sliced
1 small bunch watercress
¼ cup Greek olives
½ cup olive oil
2 tablespoons fresh lemon juice
2 tablespoons white wine vinegar
Salt and pepper to taste

1. Peel pomelos and remove flesh from membrane. Place in salad bowl with avocado, watercress, and olives.
2. Combine oil, lemon juice, and vinegar in a small bowl. Blend well, pour over salad, and toss gently. Season to taste and serve.

Prickly Pear (Fig of India)

I discovered the grotesquely handsome prickly pear, *il fico d'India*, or "Indian fig," during a visit to Sicily, my four grandparents' homeland. The cactus plant is a repeating motif all along the expanse of sensually mountainous landscape seen from long train rides over the rugged isle. The rainbow-hued fruit is prickly but not pear-shaped; it's more like an oblong egg. At dinnertime along with my cousins' homegrown meals appeared bleeding magenta slices of the very seedy and grainy-textured fruit. The busy pulp is something like watermelon, very sweet and porously juicy, but rather bland. As rampant as the fruit is in Sicily and other parts of the world, it is of sporadic appeal and appearance in this country. The swarms of black seeds, not always edible, are no doubt partially responsible for that lag.

You may see different shades of prickly pears in the marketplace. They range from lime green to cherry mauve, the latter being sweeter and tastier. They are in season from September through May. The fruit should feel gently giving, but not mushy, healthily flushed with color, and with no rot or decay. Store it in a cool, dry place. Refrigerate if keeping longer than a week.

Since the seeds may warrant slow acceptance, the best way to serve the prickly pear for the first time is as chilled slices with other fruit on a tray. If nothing else, it is ostentatious enough to encourage curious nibblings and a few conversational expletives.

For more daring treatments, peel the skin (it's usually depricked before going to market), cube the fruit, and add to fruit salad with more assertive fruits such as berries. As with pomegranates, you can retrieve the juice from the crackling pulp by squeezing it through a cloth bag or tediously rubbing it through a sieve. Add the juice to punches, cocktails, and chilled fruit soups. If you are willing to capture the juice, you are probably willing to turn it into an attractive cold soufflé or a fruit filling for baked goods. You can add the juice to sauces and syrups and even salad dressings. Like pomegranates too, prickly pears offer a noteworthy amount of potassium and vitamin C, as well as some vitamin A.

Prickly Pear Pink Squirrel

 *4 servings*

4 prickly pears, peeled
2 cups half-and-half
4 1-ounce shots Crème de Noyeaux (almond) liqueur (or any
  other nut-flavored liqueur, such as Frangelico)

Chop pears and place in blender. Add remaining ingredients
and puree on high speed. Strain and serve straight up or over ice
in tall cocktail glasses.

Quince

A symbol of the Greek and Roman ideals of love, beauty, and
fertility, the quince, a member of the rose family, is rich in ro-
mance and myth. It is the legendary golden apple of Aphrodite
and Hesperides. Its baroque lily-white to bloodred flowers provide
a common study for Eastern art. Some think the quince, native
to Asia Minor, may have been the original forbidden fruit.

If it was, I doubt the first man or woman knew enough to cook
the wood-hard raw fruit before taking the bite that cost us all
Paradise. The close-grained texture of the dry fruit requires the
chemistry of heat to bring forth its characteristic qualities.

There are several varieties of quince. The type grown in California, called *pineapple quince*, has traits of both apple and pear,
which, like the quince, are in the rose family. Its color is sunny
golden like a ripe Bartlett pear. Its odd shape is that of a rotund
pear or an elongated apple. When first picked, the quince wears

a downy coat of fuzz like a peach, but mechanical rubbing usually eliminates this furriness.

What the quince lacks in its raw texture, it more than compensates for in its pervasive cooked fragrance. Its bouquet is so appealing and seductive that in olden days the fruit was left with lavender to scent rooms for months. You can aromatize your own kitchen by leaving bowls of the fruit in a warm place or put up a bushelful of quince for the nostalgia of a once-popular jelly. The flavor of quince is a sweet mix of Asian pear and tropical fruits.

It has even more pectin (the thickening agent of jellies) than apples and is well suited for jams, candies, preserves, and marmalade.

Cook quinces as you would pears and apples and even mix the quince with them in any recipe that involves cooking. Poaching, braising, and stewing transform the hard astringent fruit into something tender, scented, and tasty. Cinnamon stick and cloves are good spices for quince compotes. Cooked quince puree is a pleasant change from applesauce, although the quince will never totally surrender all its firmness as apples do with cooking. Use the quince in fruit pies, tarts, and cake fillings, or as an accompaniment to pork and other meats or poultry.

You can cook the quince with peel, core, and all, for extracting maximum flavor, if you intend to sieve or puree afterward. A potato peeler or paring knife will easily remove the skin of the uncooked fruit, though the core may require extra elbow grease to remove. Exposed quince flesh browns like that of apples, so if you are holding the sliced fruit for a while, place it in acidulated water (about 1 tablespoon of lemon juice mixed with every cup of water needed to cover the fruit) or toss it with just lemon juice.

Select large, firm quinces, with clear, smooth yellow skin. Quinces never soften like apples and pears. Slight blemishing can be cut away. Small knobby quinces are more difficult to peel and core. The aromatic fruit keeps well, but bruises easily. Store at room temperature or refrigerate for weeks.

Hazelnut-Quince Tart

 *8 servings*

Quinces
2 pounds quinces
1/2 cup sugar
1 cinnamon stick

Pastry
1 1/2 cups flour
8 tablespoons (1 stick) unsalted butter, chilled and cut into 8
    pieces
1 tablespoon sugar
1 tablespoon ice water, or more if needed

Filling
1 cup toasted hazelnuts
1 egg
1/2 cup light cream
1/4 cup dark brown sugar
1/4 teaspoon lemon zest
1/2 teaspoon vanilla extract

1. *Prepare quinces*: Peel, halve, and core quinces. Place halves
with sugar and cinnamon stick in a large pot, cover with water,
and simmer until tender, about 40 minutes. Allow to cool in liquid
and strain.

2. *Prepare pastry*: Pulse flour, butter, and sugar in food processor
fitted with metal blade until mixture resembles oatmeal. Add water
as needed and pulse just until mixture begins to adhere into a ball,
about 10 seconds. Wrap dough in plastic and refrigerate for 1
hour.

3. *Prepare filling*: Grind nuts in food processor. Add egg, cream,
sugar, zest, and vanilla through feed tube, pulsing each ingredient

just until evenly blended in. Scrape down sides with spatula, if necessary.

4. *Assemble*: Roll two-thirds of the dough on a lightly floured surface into a 12-inch circle. Transfer to a 10-inch tart pan with a removable bottom. Press dough evenly against bottom and side of pan. Preheat oven to 400°F. Prick tart shell with a fork and bake for 10 minutes, until lightly golden. If shell begins to balloon as it bakes, prick with fork again. Allow to cool. Lower oven to 350°.

5. Cut cooled quinces into thin slices. Spread filling over cooled tart shell. Spread quince slices evenly over filling.

6. Roll out the unbaked dough to a 10½-inch circle. Lay it gently over the tart. Crimp edges to seal. With a knife, slit center of dough in a pinwheel design. Bake in lower part of oven for 25 to 30 minutes, until top is a rich golden brown and begins to puff. Let tart cool at room temperature for 1 hour or longer before cutting.

Sapodilla

In the forests of southern Mexico and parts of Central America, the small, shiny-leafed sapodilla tree grows wild. The tree is also cultivated in many parts of the tropics and in India, Southeast Asia, the West Indies, and Florida. The fruit survives the rigors of transport well and so is gaining popularity in the many colder climates to which it is exported.

Roundish and flat, the sapodilla is an imperfect oval, resembling a small potato or the furry kiwi fruit. A thin rough brownish tan skin covers the fruit. The soft flesh is rusty orange to honey-blond. Its flavor is a tender embodiment of honey, brown sugar, and

Vermont maple syrup, making this a most natural dessert fruit. The pulp may be smooth or granular, but when of good quality, it is always fragrant and melting like bananas or apricots. A clump of central seeds with menacing hooks must be removed, an easy task, before eating.

Ironically, the same tree that bears this delicate fruit encourages one of America's more bovine customs—gum chewing. The sapodilla tree exudes a milklike latex that provides chicle for our Chiclet and other varieties of gum.

Fortunately, the fruit has more gastronomical grace than the tree's gooey secretion. You can carve the sapodilla into wedges or scoop out the spoonable flesh, as desired. The sweet, subtle fruit may benefit from a dash of lime juice. Coconut and a splash of rum is a popular balmy-climate treatment for the fruit. Or add the slices to salads or vegetable-fruit platters. In tropical climates fruited grains tend to be common sustenance. Cooked rice with chunks of sapodilla, lemon zest, and fresh ginger is a delicious and healthful meal.

When the pulp is too soft to slice, mash it for use in pudding and custard or muffins and other quickbreads. The date-sweet flesh is a natural base for all the frozen cream confections, and sapodilla ice cream is a favorite in Central America. Molasses-tinted, the flesh is perfect for an English pudding called *fool*, made with fruit, cream, lemon or other flavoring, and custard.

Select fruit that is somewhat soft and smooth—too hard can indicate an unpleasant gritty interior. Until fully ripened, the fruit is inedible, being too astringent. Left at room temperature, hard fruit will soften to good taste and texture, like most tropical fruits. To check for readiness, scratch the fuzzy skin with your fingernail. If it shows green, the fruit is not ready; if yellow, it is ripe. Chill ripe fruit for several days.

Sapodilla and Saffron Rice

 *8 servings*

2 teaspoons saffron threads
4 cups boiling water
4 tablespoons (½ stick) butter
2 cups long grain brown rice
½ teaspoon salt
2 large sapodillas
¼ cup golden raisins
½ cup toasted almond slivers
½ teaspoon cinnamon
¼ teaspoon ground cloves

1. Soak saffron in ¼ cup of the boiling water for 10 minutes.

2. Melt butter in a large skillet. Add rice and stir until evenly coated with butter. Cook for 5 minutes over low heat. Stir in remaining hot water and salt, and bring to a boil over high heat. Add saffron with its water and stir gently. Reduce heat, cover, and let simmer for 25 to 30 minutes, until rice has absorbed all of the liquid and is tender.

3. Peel and seed sapodillas. Chop into ½-inch pieces. Stir sapodilla into rice along with raisins, almonds, cinnamon, and cloves. Let stand 5 minutes, then serve.

Tamarillo

The tamarillo resembles a tie-dyed Easter egg that sprouted a long wiry wood stem. Its flaming red brilliance imposed over its golden yellow underglow gives this fruit a mosaic appearance. This aspect continues on the moist fleshy inside, where its complexion of dewy pêche melba is offset by curls of soft blood-amber seeds.

Also known as the *tree tomato*, the tamarillo grows on a tall shrub that was cultivated for years by Peruvian Indians. New Zealand now gives us our supply of tamarillos. The florid fruit is also grown in Kenya.

The ovoid tamarillo, though beautifully sensuous, seems to have an identity crisis. Is it a fruit or a vegetable? Its botanical ambivalence is not unlike our garden-variety tomato, which is classified as fruit, but used as vegetable. In fact, its taste, which is not fruit-sweet, has the sour notes of tomatoes, the subtlety of cooked carrots, and the slight punch of wintergreen. Call it a sweet vegetable or a sour fruit, as you like.

The tamarillo, a member of the eggplant family, has a tender meaty flesh best suited for cooking. Its ambiguous nature lends the adaptable veggie-fruit to sweet dessert and savory vegetable preparations. The tamarillo can be eaten raw, but cooking brings out its best aspects. The thin red-and-yellow skin is tough and inedible and easily pulled off. Acidic and/or salty condiments, such as vinegar, lemon juice, soy or Worcestershire sauce, and herbs, such as basil and parsley, emphasize one role. Sugars, honey, syrups, cinnamon, and nutmeg bring the other side of its personality to the fore. One way to eat this radiant fruit out of hand is by cutting it in half widthwise, seasoning it as desired, and spooning the pulp out of its palm-size ramekin shape.

Tamarillos are a summer and fall fruit. Use the same selection principles for tamarillos as you would for tomatoes: a firm, heavy fruit with taut skin and attractive color (the more predominant the yellow tones, the sweeter and milder the fruit). The hard fruit will ripen at room temperature; its fragrant wintergreen scent will assert itself and the skin, when pressed, will feel pliant like a midway-ripe tomato. Chill the fruit before eating it raw. Store in the refrigerator for seven to ten days. You can peel, slice, and freeze the fruit (or puree it first) for up to six months. The semisweet flesh can be made into jellies, jams, preserves, chutneys, and relishes.

The tamarillo's duality makes it a versatile ingredient. It goes with meat and fowl entrées or with all manner of dessert interpretation. Its dense pudding flesh can be made into custard, pie and cake filling, or a syrupy compote. Try pairing the vivid fruit slices with other fruits, experimenting with combinations that please your palate. The vitamin-A- and -C-enriched fruit served with cottage cheese is a refreshing, eye-tempting variation on a low-calorie theme.

Honey-Baked Tamarillos

 *4 servings*

6 tamarillos
¼ cup light honey
2 tablespoons fresh lime juice
Yogurt
Fresh mint leaves

Preheat oven to 350°F. Peel tamarillos and slice into round ¼-inch disks. Arrange in a baking dish and drizzle with honey and lime juice. Bake 20 minutes until tender. Serve garnished with yogurt and mint leaves; serve alone, as an accompaniment to lamb, or with cake, ice cream, or other dessert.

Tamarind

The tamarind (from the Arabic *tamrhindi*, meaning "Indian date") is a funny-looking, caterpillar-shaped fruit (or pod) from a leguminous tropical tree. The tree originated in the savanna zone of Africa and made its way to India during ancient times. The garish tree, with its hard yellow wood, red-striped yellow flowers, plumed leaves, and brown leathery pods, is a real jack-of-all-trades. It shares its culinary usefulness with commercial, herbal, and industrial circles. The same tree that yields this world-renowned spicy fruit flavoring also contributes the following: a sturdy wood glue, industrial-strength tartaric acid, gunpowder from its charcoal-burned wood, a red dye, a silver and brass cleaner, a cooling laxative, not to mention the informal use of the fruit's alleged aphrodisiac attributes.

Its odd jobs aside, the tamarind is one of the most popular flavors in fruit drinks and desserts throughout India, Mexico, the Caribbean, and other tropical areas of the world. The brittle, cinnamon-colored pods range from 3 to 8 inches long, looking like dark carob beans. A very sticky acid pulp, which surrounds from one to twelve shiny brown seeds, resides within. The chocolate-brown pulp and seeds are steeped in hot water until they relinquish their spicy acid flavor. The liquid is then sweetened for a sprightly beverage as universally appealing as lemonade.

The concentrated tangy fruit flavoring also has many other applications. It is regarded highly as a seasoning for meats, fish, vegetables, Indian *dhal* (a puree of dried peas or lentils), curries, and chutneys. Its bite is a secret, but indispensable, ingredient in Worcestershire sauce.

The sweetened tamarind pulp (made by soaking the whole pods overnight, then removing the seeds from the softened pulp) is the most common way to infuse the exotic fruit into dessert recipes, such as tamarind sherbet, ice cream, or mousse. You may also want to sieve the pulp for smoother texture.

The tamarind is available in at least two forms: as pods or as cakes of pulp and seed. (You may also come across tamarind extract, sold in small tubs.) Food shops specializing in Indian foods are the best places to find tamarind products. If buying pods, avoid broken ones. You can preserve tamarind indefinitely by pressing the shelled pulp into cakes, wrapping it in plastic, and storing it in a cool place.

Tamarind Cooler

¼ pound tamarinds
6 cups water
½ cup sugar

Place tamarinds in large bowl, cover with water, and soak overnight. Strain and reserve soaking liquid. Strain seeds out of pulp and add pulp back to soaking liquid. Stir in sugar. Serve chilled over ice.

Ugli Fruit

From the festive isle of Jamaica and related to the grapefruit comes the ugli fruit (sounding more like OO-gli, in the Jamaican dialect). It is not the inner pink-golden flesh that warrants the rather direct epithet of a name, but the unevenly knobbed rind of mottled green orange. Although the ugli fruit is definitely a hybrid, it's as if the grapefruit and the tangerine who may have sired this pathetic sight fought to keep their own genetic traits clearly visible. The homely fruit has few seeds, packs more juice than the grapefruit, and like the pomelo can be used in any way the grapefruit is. The flavor unites hints of orange and grapefruit, with minor notes of other citrus.

Its dazzling tart-sweet disposition makes up for a multitude of sins in the looks department. The vitamin-C-rich ugli fruit can be refreshing and enjoyable as a grapefruit, peeled and segmented. It is accommodating most anywhere other citrus fruits are. Candied peel and marmalade are not beyond the scope of this offspring of a mixed marriage.

The inner membrane-covered pulp separates easily from its loose-fitting rind and pith. The hybrid action is no doubt responsible for the pulpy flesh, which is actually a mesh of juice-swollen "hairs."

Select ugli fruit that are firm and heavy like good grapefruit, indicating a high juice content. Uneven coloring and some brown spotting are normal. The fruit stores very well. Keep as you would grapefruit, at room temperature or in the refrigerator.

Honey-Glazed Ugli Fruit

 *4 servings*

3 large ugli fruit
½ cup honey
1 cup crème fraîche or sour cream
4 sprigs fresh mint

1. Remove ugli fruit from rind, pith, and membrane. Slice in half or thirds if very large. Dip each piece of fruit in honey to coat well, arrange in one layer on baking sheet. Broil under pre-heated broiler about 5 inches from heat for 3 to 5 minutes, until fruit is translucent.

2. Divide sections among 4 dessert plates, arranging pinwheel fashion. Spoon crème fraîche over each serving and garnish with fresh mint.

White Sapote

There are several fruits with distinctly differing characteristics, native to Mexico and Central America, all called *sapote* (or *sapota*), the Spanish word referring to soft fruit—the one trait shared by all. For clarity's sake the fruits are distinguished as white (*Casimiroa edulis*) or black (*Diospyros ebenaster, retz*). Their scientific names may be used when confusion takes over. To add to the befuddlement, green and yellow sapotes also exist.

It is the white sapote, grown in small quantities in California and Florida, whose future prospects look rosiest for grand-scale marketing. Right now it is the most commercially available of the sapote bunch. Its highly coveted flesh is sweet and creamy, a dead ringer for a carefully prepared custard. Its musky vanilla flavor with strains of peach and banana has been compared to that of a sweetened avocado. Known also as "the peach of the tropics," the fruit is about 2½ inches in diameter and contains several ovoid pits, resembling a green apple in shape and color.

To eat the delicate fruit, peel the skin off and extricate the pits from the pale flesh. Enjoyed alone or with other fruit, the white sapote needs little adornment. It can also be pureed and made into a fancier dessert, such as pie or mousse, custard, creams, and any frozen dessert.

Look for firm fruit, with no bruises, in summer. Allow to ripen at room temperature until it is marshmallow soft, an overnight phenomenon with this precocious fruit. Chill to keep longer.

Sapote Blanco Mousse

 *Makes 5 to 6 cups*

1¼ cups mashed ripe white sapote pulp
¼ cup extrafine sugar
1 teaspoon vanilla extract
3 tablespoons brandy
½ pint heavy cream, whipped
Shaved chocolate

Combine sapote, sugar, vanilla, and brandy. Fold in whipped cream. Spoon mixture into 6 parfait glasses and garnish with shaved chocolate. Chill until ready to serve.

VEGETABLES

Like fruits, vegetables supply the body with a mother lode of nutrition, in addition to being rich in fiber and low in calories. Such accolades are no less merited for the items here that may appear new to many of us. Add high doses of iron and calcium to the roster of important nutrients that many vegetables, green ones in particular, contribute.

These vegetables are versatile, too. Many require little or no cooking, making perfect raw salad ingredients. Again, the selection, storage, and preparation information is intended to help you maximize taste and nutrition for each vegetable. Since there are a good number of leafy green vegetables with similar cleaning and storage requirements, I've described those steps up front here for easy referral.

CLEANING AND STORING GREENS

Nothing beats a fresh green in peak condition for taste, visual appeal, and nutrition. Here are some basic tips for keeping your greens that way. Follow these guidelines for storing the greens discussed, unless advised otherwise.

Never wash greens before storing them, since moisture promotes decay and can affect the content of water-soluble nutrients. To protect leafy greens from moisture already on them, wrap them in a couple of layers of paper toweling, then in perforated (or open-ended) plastic. Store in the vegetable crisper of the refrigerator. Although some greens remain crisp longer than others, your best bet for ideal taste, texture, and nutrition is to use them all within three to five days.

Just before cooking greens, rinse them thoroughly in cold water to clean. Do not soak the greens, as this will leach out soluble nutrients, too. Drain them in a colander if cooking, or dry more thoroughly in a lettuce spin-dryer. The residual water from washing is enough to steam the greens, over low heat, in a tightly covered pot.

Amaranth Greens

Although it is the grain or seed that is the primary harvest of the amaranth plant, the young leaves also have substantial culinary and nutritional stature.

The history of amaranth, a food that harks back six thousand years, is tied closely to that of the Aztec Indians in Mexico. The Aztecs not only worked the phenomenally nutritious plant into their diet, but also worked it into their religious ceremonies in the form of a sweet, mixed occasionally with a bit of human blood. The grain fell from grace at the hands of the conqueror Cortéz, who banished the plant's use and the pagan rituals in which it figured. The Christian Spaniards stomped the plant into oblivion, until recent times.

The nutritional profile of amaranth makes it easy to understand its appeal to the health-minded. According to the editors of *Organic Gardening and Farming* (in *Unusual Vegetables*, Rodale, 1978), "The raw greens have substantially more calcium than beet greens, kale, chard, and spinach, and more iron than all these leaf vegetables and collards as well. . . . Researchers have declared it [amaranth] an outstanding source of leaf protein concentrates that can be used as fodder or as human food."

The greens taste something like spinach, with more assertive pepperiness. The stems, tasting more like artichokes, may be tough if too mature. If you are a greens fancier, the best way to try amaranth is first steamed until tender (about 10 minutes), then briefly sautéed in oil (preferably a fragrant olive oil) with garlic. Or try it with hot bacon dressing. You can use amaranth in every way you would spinach or other greens—in quiches, omelets, or any egg-cheese concoction, in casseroles, vegetable medleys, and in soups, whole or as a puree base.

The selection and keeping qualities of amaranth greens, harvested in the summer, are similar to those of spinach. Refrigerate them, wrapped in paper toweling, for several days. You can also blanch and freeze the greens for several months.

Amaranth Greens with Sweet-and-Sour Bacon Dressing

 *4 to 6 servings*

This is an especially good accompaniment to roasted chicken, veal cutlets, or beef entrées.

1½ pounds amaranth greens
3 strips bacon
¼ cup finely minced onion
1 cup meat or vegetable stock
2 tablespoons sweet sherry
2 tablespoons cider vinegar
1 teaspoon sugar

¼ teaspoon ground coriander
Salt and pepper to taste

1. Steam greens until tender, about 15 to 20 minutes. Set aside.
2. Meanwhile, fry bacon slowly until crisp. Add onion during last 7 minutes of cooking. Drain off all but about 2 tablespoons of fat. Stir in remaining ingredients.
3. Chop greens slightly and toss with dressing. Serve immediately.

Arugula (Roquette)

I first tasted this piquant green, rich in vitamins A and C and minerals iron and calcium, as a component of a simple mixed green salad. Its lively bite severed forever my ties with insipid iceberg lettuce. Slightly bitter and robust, its poignantly herby flavor gently awash in a vinaigrette is reminiscent of a mellow horseradish. It will do wonders for the American salad bowl and possibly the salad bar someday as it gains popularity.

Commonly called *rocket* (or *roquette*), arugula is popular in Italy, where it pairs famously with radicchio (see page 119), and grows wild in Europe. It is a crucifer vegetable, a member of the cabbage clan, and as a wild weed, its pungency can become overwhelming. I grow the cultivated type in my garden and use it in a fifty-fifty blend with any mild leaf lettuce. You can't mistake the heady aroma of arugula. It reminds me of sun-baked wild herbs I've sniffed on nature trails high in the Rockies. It is profusely earthy and herby.

You can usually find the audacious green all year round in markets that carry unusual produce. It appears in small bunches, often with its earth-covered roots and its long frayed leaves somewhat like those on a head of broccoli but more emerald in color. The leaves should appear healthy, not wilted or damaged. Cut the roots away and rinse the grit off carefully before using. A salad spinner is a good device for removing the moisture. Store as you would spinach.

You can savor arugula in hot or cold salads with other greens. Its spicy bite goes well with balsamic vinegar and hazelnut oil or lemon juice and olive oil dressings. Red onions, avocado, and sautéed wild mushrooms are appealing and complementary flavors. Arugula can also enliven omelets, soups, pasta dishes, casseroles, or other steamed vegetables.

Arugula, Swiss, and Onion Omelet or Crêpe Filling

 *4 servings*

enough filling for 4 2-egg omelets, 8 small crêpes, or 4 large crêpes

2 tablespoons sweet butter
½ cup chopped scallions
1 small bunch (about ½ pound) cleaned arugula leaves
½ pound cleaned spinach leaves
2 cups grated Swiss cheese

1. Melt butter and add scallions. Cook until soft, about 5 minutes.

2. Turn heat to low. Place arugula and spinach on top of scallions, cover pan, and steam until greens are wilted, about 3 minutes. Transfer to bowl. Mix and chop greens slightly with a knife and fork.

3. If making omelets, divide mixture into 4 portions, adding ½ cup cheese to each omelet along with filling. If making crêpes

divide filling and cheese accordingly, then place the crêpes in a chafing dish and heat in moderate oven, 325°F., until cheese is melted. Serve crêpes with Béchamel Sauce, if desired (see below).

Béchamel Sauce for Crêpes

 *Makes 1 cup*

1 tablespoon butter
1 tablespoon flour
1 cup milk or cream
2 tablespoons grated Parmesan
¼ teaspoon salt
¼ teaspoon grated nutmeg

Melt butter in a small saucepan over low heat. Stir in flour until absorbed evenly. Pour milk or cream into roux very slowly, constantly stirring until sauce is thickened, about 10 to 15 minutes. Stir in cheese and cook 3 minutes longer. Add salt and nutmeg. Pour over crêpes before or after heating.

Hazelnut Oil Dressing for Arugula Salad

 *Makes ¾ cup*

I developed this recipe for the *New York Times* Living Section, July 16, 1986. It goes well with a salad mixed with arugula, redleaf lettuce, watercress, avocado, and red onions.

1 clove garlic
¼ cup balsamic vinegar
¼ cup hazelnut oil
¼ cup virgin olive oil

Cut garlic in half and combine with vinegar and oils in a small bowl. Stir gently and set aside for 1 to 2 hours. Remove garlic before tossing salad with dressing.

Belgian Endive

Grown almost exclusively in Belgium, Belgian endive is considered a root chicory (though it is not a root) that actually results from growing escarole (both the same *Cichorium endivia* species) in a certain way. Both Belgian endive and escarole start out from the same exact seed. But endive, also called *Witloof* (Flemish for "white leaf") or *barbe-de-bouc* ("goat's beard"), becomes a furled bunch of blanched leaves when the plants are sequestered in total darkness for a while just before going to market. This natural bleaching method deprives the leaves of the light-dependent green chlorophyll you see in all plant life. The pigment-deprived leaves are tender yet crisp, and a salad bowl ingredient much sought after by gourmet cooks today. The inner hearts are especially favored for their unique clean, bitterish flavor.

A cold-weather vegetable, endive is in peak form during the winter and fall. The creamy white spike of a head should be tightly wrapped, with pale yellow tinting only at the very edges of the leaves. Photosynthesis will occur with exposure to light, developing the leaf-green pigment, which means a change in the characteristic delicate flavor. The endive is often wrapped in purple tissue paper to avoid this greening reaction to light. Avoid greened or browned heads as they are an indication of aging.

Store Belgian endive wrapped in a brown paper bag to minimize exposure to light, in the refrigerator, for not more than two days.

An aristocrat of the salad bowl, endive can elevate the status of a few ordinary greens. Mustard vinaigrettes and *à la grecque* dressing make good endive enhancements. A crumbling of any of the blue cheeses, walnuts, apples, and pears are equally effective complements for endive in salads and on appetizer trays. The ashen leaves may be cooked too; remove the bitter cone-shaped base first. The French and Belgians braise and serve them with ham. A velvety cream sauce can turn the tender cooked vegetable into elegant sustenance. It can be made into a successful au gratin, too.

Creamy Endive-Carrot Soup

 *4 servings*

2 tablespoons butter
½ cup chopped scallions
3½ cups chopped endive
3 carrots, peeled and sliced
2 cups meat or vegetable stock
2 cups half-and-half
¼ teaspoon salt
½ teaspoon black pepper
¼ teaspoon nutmeg
Few sprigs of watercress or mint leaves

1. Heat butter in a large saucepan. Add scallions, endive, and carrots. Sauté, stirring occasionally, for 10 minutes. Add stock, bring to a boil, then reduce heat, cover, and simmer for 5 minutes. Allow to cool.
2. Puree cooled mixture in several batches, if necessary. Return puree to saucepan. Add half-and-half, salt, pepper, and nutmeg. Reheat, but do not boil. Ladle into bowls and garnish each serving with watercress or mint leaves.

Boniato

Also called *batata*, *white sweet potato*, and *camote*, the boniato is very similar in appearance and taste to our American sweet potato of Thanksgiving fame. This ruddy, pink-skinned tuber is a bit tubbier, though, and its interior white flesh a bit drier—more like that of a regular white potato. Lower in calories than our sweet potato, it is the root vegetable of choice in tropical America, where it has been popular for ages.

Although it is not a complete protein (meaning it lacks some of the essential amino acids that our bodies cannot synthesize), the boniato is a protein food. This, along with its high starch content, no doubt accounts for its being a staple in countries where animal protein is not so abundant as in the United States. As a complex carbohydrate, the boniato, like all our other potatoes, should be of interest to anyone in want of a high-energy diet. This type of carbohydrate (also prominent in pasta, rice, and bread) is what athletes eat to keep going for the long haul. As a starch food, boniato is filling, totally fat- and cholesterol-free, and by no means an empty-calorie food. A one-half-cup serving has about 120 calories as well as 210 milligrams of potassium, an especially important mineral to replenish if you are physically active. Boniato fits in perfectly with the trend of making a potato the centerpiece of a meal, nestled beneath a substantial sauce or topping.

The boniato can be all that its orange and white counterparts are—baked, candied, boiled, mashed, pureed. On the islands where it is a common food, people are as fond as we are of turning the potato into chips. Added to soups or stews, its delicate nutty flavor will sweeten the pot. The skin of baked boniato is delicious and, like other potatoes, most of its plentiful vitamins A and C are concentrated just under the skin.

The boniato is generally available year round, usually in markets carrying Latin foods. Select firm, smooth-skinned vegetables with minimal blemishing and no mold. You can peel them with a peeler, as you would any potato. Store as you would potatoes, too—never in the refrigerator, but in the potato bin or any cool, dry, dark place.

Orange Baked Boniato with Maple Buttermilk Dressing

 *4 servings*

4 medium-size boniatos
3 tablespoons butter
¼ cup orange juice
¾ cup buttermilk
2 tablespoons maple syrup
1 teaspoon orange zest
¼ teaspoon cinnamon
4 sprigs fresh mint leaves

1. Preheat oven to 375°F. Scrub boniatos clean and dry. Bake for 1 hour, or until tender through when pierced with a fork.

2. When cool enough to handle, slice top off each boniato. Scrape pulp from inside and place in food processor fitted with metal blade. Add butter, juice, and ¼ cup of buttermilk, and process until smooth.

3. Refill boniato shells with mixture. If mixture has cooled too much, reheat filled boniatos in 375° oven for about 10 minutes.

4. Combine remaining buttermilk, syrup, zest, and cinnamon. Pour some over each boniato and place remaining dressing in small pitcher. Garnish each boniato with mint leaves.

Broccoli Rabe

Italians love their greens—bitter, sweet, tender, chewy, raw, and cooked. Broccoli rabe (or raab) is one of those greens at last making an appearance in the culinary mainstream. But my grandparents and parents have always cooked it, for as long as I can remember. I always thought of this green as a vegetable that really wanted to be broccoli—though the way my grandmother steeped broccoli rabe in a fruity olive oil that contained several well-browned toes of garlic, it was much better than broccoli.

Broccoli rabe is also called *turnip broccoli*, a loose translation of its Italian title *broccolini de rapa*. Many species come from the old country thanks to the nostalgia of Italian-American gardeners.

Not part of the broccoli group at all, broccoli rabe is the tender shoot of a wintered-over turnip plant. It is a deep evergreen color like broccoli, but with thinner stalks, about the diameter of your pinkie finger, and from 10 to 18 inches long. It has frill-edged leaves with florets that slightly resemble broccoli's tight buds. One could easily pass this plant over as a weed.

Some say broccoli rabe is bitter. However, it's not bitter the way escarole or dandelion can be, but is more pungent. For me it has hints of spinach, broccoli, collards, and mustard greens with pleasant sour or tart notes.

No matter what you intend to do with broccoli rabe, steam it first, slowly and just until it is tender (though my grandmother always overcooked it, and it was fine). Its color should still be a vivid green. Then you can sauté it with oil, puree it for a soup, or chop it for use in omelets and frittatas. Sometimes the stalks' ends are a little tough; just cut them away after they're cooked. My favorite way to enjoy this robust vegetable is steamed with a drizzle of olive oil and a squirt of lemon juice and fresh ground pepper. If I am feeling ambitious I may turn a batch into a baked frittata with Swiss and Parmesan cheeses and tomatoes. Broccoli rabe would be right with a pasta primavera variation. In fact, a little tomato sauce enhances its already noteworthy nutrition. The vitamin C in tomatoes helps make the abundant minerals calcium and iron in greens such as broccoli rabe more available to your body (otherwise these minerals are inhibited by oxalic acid, a substance in the green that binds with them). In addition, broccoli rabe has its own profusion of vitamins A and C and a good amount of potassium.

Broccoli rabe is available from early fall through spring. The leaves should be dark forest green, succulent looking, not wilted, and the stalks shouldn't be too fat or they'll be tough. There may be some flowering buds, but most should be closed. Store like other greens (see page 54).

Broccoli Rabe, Italian-Style

 *2 to 4 servings*

This simple treatment is by far the best way to enjoy this green.

1 pound broccoli rabe
¼ cup fruity olive oil
2 to 3 cloves garlic, chopped
2 to 3 tablespoons fresh lemon juice
Salt and freshly ground pepper to taste

1. Clean greens and cut off tough stem ends. Steam until tender, about 20 minutes.
2. Heat oil in a large skillet. Add garlic and cook until just lightly brown. Add broccoli rabe, toss, and cook just until heated through. Toss with lemon juice, salt, and pepper, and serve.

Suggestions: Chop and add to omelets, frittatas, or quiche fillings.

Burdock

A good friend and I know well one of burdock's less desirable traits. Burdock is the devil of a prickly plant that embedded its burrs in our socks and running shoes as we ran over wilderness trails in the canyons and mountains of northern Utah. For, although its cultivated variety has gastronomical worth, left to its own devices the plant grows wild and is known as both an irksome weed and a medicinal herb.

Burdock's alluring side owes to the Japanese domestication of this mischievous plant, which they call *gobo* or *takinogawa*. They treasure its roots for their gustatory delicacy and blood-purifying benefits. Burdock is said also to be a good treatment for aching joints and skin disorders. According to herbalist writers Gaea and Shandor Weiss, Hawaiians credit burdock "with an ability to increase strength and endurance." To get them through tough tasks, Hawaiians repeat "I need gobo" over and over again.

Burdock roots look like long gnarly cream-beige carrots or parsnips, but they are more fibrous in texture. To prepare burdock, scrape or peel the outer layer down to the lighter flesh. Slice the root into thin lozenge shapes, diagonals, or julienne strips. Soak the cut vegetable in acidulated water (1 tablespoon of lemon juice or vinegar for each cup of water) until ready to cook, as exposure to air turns the white flesh to tarnished gray rather quickly. The Japanese, whose traditional cuisine is a paradigm of restraint, simply add burdock slices to clear soup broth or sauté it with a dash of soy sauce. Its sweet flavor and crunchy-firm texture are the highlight of a dish. Burdock has a health-food aura that makes it seem most natural with other steamed or stir-fried vegetables, tofu, and brown rice.

Its earthiness does not belie its appearance. You'll often find the taproot in fall and winter in natural-food and Oriental stores, with a good layer of its soil bed intact, a very healthy state. It should be firm and crisp like a fresh carrot, not limp and bendable like an old one. Store burdock for a few days at most, wrapped in a damp cloth or paper towel in the refrigerator.

Sesame Chicken Stir-Fry with Burdock

 *4 servings*

½ cup soy sauce
2 tablespoons cider vinegar
2 tablespoons sherry
2 teaspoons minced garlic
1 tablespoon minced fresh ginger
1 teaspoon crushed red pepper
1 pound skinless boned chicken breasts cut into 1-inch cubes
2 tablespoons peanut oil
1 large red bell pepper cut into thin strips
1½ cups thinly sliced burdock
1 cup broccoli florets
1 tablespoon cornstarch
2 teaspoons dark sesame oil
2 tablespoons toasted sesame seeds
4 scallions, trimmed and thinly sliced

1. In a shallow bowl combine soy sauce, vinegar, sherry, garlic, ginger, crushed pepper, and chicken. Allow to marinate at least 1 hour, stirring occasionally.

2. Heat wok over high heat, then add the peanut oil and heat until a scallion ring sizzles in the oil. Add red bell pepper, burdock, and broccoli and cook, stirring often, for 2 minutes.

3. Drain chicken and reserve marinade. Add chicken to wok and toss until cooked through, about 7 minutes.

4. Stir cornstarch into marinade. Add to wok and stir to coat

all ingredients. Cook 1 minute longer, just until the sauce thickens.

5. Remove wok from heat. Drizzle sesame oil over mixture. Add sesame seeds and scallions and toss. Serve immediately with steaming hot rice or buckwheat noodles.

Cardoon

One nation's weed is another's vegetable. This double-identity plant may well inspire such a proverb. In my family it has been known to inspire real-life drama, as hoarding this southern Italian favorite is not unheard of. I have heard of old Italians who know where cardoons grow wild, but who wouldn't on their lives share the information with the community.

To the world at large, cardoon, with its long, wide, celerylike stems, is an innocuous weed. The delicacy of this lime-green thistle-stalked vegetable eludes most. But my mother tells me how the old-timers in Peterstown, the Italian neighborhood of Elizabeth, New Jersey, where she grew up, once hawked these cherished weeds in the open-air market that still exists. "In the spring the old ladies went into the fields, then they would come to the market and to our houses with bundles of cardoons wrapped in cloths and aprons, balanced on their heads."

No one has summoned forth the cardoon's attributes the way my father's mother once did. For many years I thought she was serving us *God-dunes*, the way she pronounced the vegetable. She boiled the stems first (as you must always) in salted water, for about 20 to 25 minutes, until chewy-tender. She then cut them into 4-inch strips, dipped three or four at a time in egg, then seasoned bread crumbs and Parmesan, and fried them in olive oil.

The result was the first of many foods that reminded me of veal cutlets, but better and more complex.

The plant's goodness resides in its juicy chardlike stalks, which possess mushroom and asparagus sweetness laced with escarole bitterness. Also called *thistle artichoke*, cardoon is a predecessor to the globe artichoke, and the flavor is similar to that vegetable's. The texture is meaty and chewy. Other Mediterranean cooks, as well as the Italians, revere cardoon (its name derives from the French word *chardon*, "thistle"). There is a wild type and a cultivated one, which at a couple of feet in length looks like an oversized head of spiny celery.

You won't find cardoons on the menu in any restaurant just yet, though I've seen them sold with the "enlightened" fare at New York City's store Balducci's, in the deli. A small supply of cardoons is grown in California. You may be able to find them in some Italian markets from spring through winter. Or you may have an Italian old-timer connection, as I do (my father's friends' stand in the outdoor market in Elizabeth at Second and Center streets), who can hustle you a good batch. Look for long, wide stalks that are a duller green than celery and not quite as stiff, but more flexible like cabbage or chard. The smaller the stalks, the more tender. Sometimes, if she had a tough bunch, my grandmother peeled away fibrous strings that she called "nerves" down the length of the stalk.

Besides making ersatz veal cutlets, you can poach cardoons in stock and dress them with oil and vinegar or lemon juice. My mother says they were commonly served this way with fava beans in her Italian neighborhood. Or, for a more refined side dish, try a seasoned mayonnaise, or a cream sauce, such as a béchamel or velouté. I've never heard of eating this iron-rich green in the raw.

Grandma Cusumano's Cardoon Cutlets

 *Makes about 1 to 1½ dozen*

1½ to 2 pounds cardoons
1 teaspoon salt
3 to 4 large eggs
1 to 1½ cups Italian seasoned bread crumbs
Olive oil for frying

1. Clean cardoons and remove any tough stalk ends. Bring a couple of quarts of water and salt to a boil. Drop in cardoons. Cook until tender, about 20 to 25 minutes. Drain and allow to cool. Slice into 4-inch strips.

2. Beat eggs in shallow bowl. Place bread crumbs in another shallow bowl.

3. Heat about ⅛-inch layer of oil in a large heavy skillet. Depending on width of cardoon stalks, take 3 or 4 at a time with a fork. Dip into egg first, then into bread crumbs and immediately into hot oil. Fry on both sides until golden brown. Add oil to pan as necessary. Place cutlets on double thickness of paper toweling to drain. You can save and reheat any leftover cutlets.

Cassava (Yucca, Manioc)

To the developed world cassava has been virtually unknown, though its by-product, tapioca, a highly digestible dessert thickener, has been used for years. Cassava is the large starchy tuber of the plant *Manihot esculenta*, native to Brazil. Its lack of renown in the developed world is more than compensated for in the other half of the world, where it is a popular staple. The people of Central

America, Africa, Asia, and the Caribbean find many uses for the starchy, filling vegetable that is a mainstay in their diet.

Cassavas have scaly barklike skin that must be peeled to reveal the white, hard, dense flesh beneath. There are over one hundred varieties, and the vegetable can be up to a foot long and about 3 to 4 inches in diameter.

Cassava's high starch content leads to a glutenous cooked texture with a sweet, bland, and mildly nutty flavor that not everyone likes. Like other similar high-carbohydrate vegetables, the cassava is extremely versatile. It can be simply boiled, baked, or fried like potatoes. It can be the starchy element in soups or stews, where it'll soak up spiciness like a sponge. The flesh can be grated fresh or cooked, and pureed. The pulp is made into many side dishes, from dumplings to fritters and puddings, just as potato and squashes are. In countries where the tuber is a mainstay, cassava is ground into a meal that is often made into a popular bread.

Cassavas are most likely to be found in markets that have a Latin neighborhood nearby. The scruffy bark covering protects the creamy white flesh and should not be soft, rotting, or cracked in many places. The first cassava I ever bought looked fine from external appearances. When I got it home and halved it, the flesh was gray and rotting. Had I sniffed the vegetable at the store I'd have detected this defect. So make sure the cassava you purchase is sweet-smelling, too. Store cassava in the refrigerator and use it within three to four days. You can also slice, wrap, and freeze cassava indefinitely.

Cassava with Salsa de Chili Rojo

 *4 to 6 servings*

Serve this as a very filling side dish.

2 to 3 pounds cassava (about 2 large ones)

For the Salsa de Chili Rojo
1 tablespoon ground dried chili, preferably
   ancho chili (see page 138)
3 Anaheim chilies, roasted, peeled, seeded,
   and finely chopped
2 pounds plum tomatoes (about 7), chopped
⅓ cup chopped onions
3 tablespoons olive oil
2 teaspoons minced garlic
1 teaspoon sugar
1 tablespoon red wine vinegar
2 tablespoons chopped fresh cilantro
1 teaspoon dried oregano
½ teaspoon ground cumin
¼ teaspoon salt
¼ teaspoon black pepper

1. Cut cassavas widthwise into 2 or 3 pieces. Slit skin with a paring knife, then peel off by hand. Place the cassava in a pot, cover with cold water. Simmer for about 15 to 20 minutes. Cassava is done when it is easily pierced with a fork. Drain when done.

2. Prepare salsa while cassava cooks. Puree ground chili with fresh chilies, tomatoes, and onions in a blender or food processor.

3. Heat oil in a large skillet. Add pureed ingredients, garlic, and sugar. Cook over moderate heat until sauce thickens, about 10 minutes. Add vinegar, cilantro, oregano, cumin, salt, and pepper and simmer 5 minutes longer.

4. Place cooked cassava in a serving dish and pour salsa over top. Serve immediately.

CASSAVA BAKED WITH CHEESE AND SALSA: Place cooked cassava in an ovenproof baking dish or pan. Pour salsa over top. Spread 1 cup grated cheddar or Monterey Jack cheese over this. Bake in a 375°F. oven for a few minutes, until cheese is melted and bubbly. Serve immediately.

Celeriac (Celery Root)

Leave it to the French to take unkempt, shaggy-looking plant life such as celeriac and turn it into an exquisitely elegant and delicious appetizer, worthy of their own high standards. Julienned into a crisp heap along with purple beets and orange carrots, it makes a colorful array like an artist's palette under a mantle of creamy saffron-colored remoulade.

In its unclean, unshaven state celeriac is a swollen and fleshy tuberous root, resembling a misshapen turnip. A profusion of smaller roots protrude from the bottom of the gnarled knob, making the whole thing look like an offspring of E.T., everyone's favorite extraterrestrial. Also called *celery root, knob celery*, and *turnip-rooted celery*, the scraggly brown root is a variety of the familiar stalk celery. It is actually the swollen stem base of the plant that interests us, not the green upper parts. Not surprisingly, the inner pristine flesh has a pronounced celery taste, though filled out with a starchier, creamier texture.

According to Jack Murdich, author of *Buying Produce* (Hearst Books, 1986), celeriac "is not one of our more popular vegetables, perhaps because it resembles an unwashed horseradish root." It is most unfortunate for our palates that we Americans are so quick to discredit foodstuffs solely on appearance.

My first encounter with this succulent tuber was as the most memorable first course of an excellent meal in the San Francisco bistro Le Candide. I wondered for the life of me why the delicate matchsticks tossed with the lemony-mustard dressing were not more prominent in American cooking. According to Georgeanne Brennan, Isaac Cronin, and Charlotte Glenn, authors of the *New American Vegetable Cookbook* (Aris Books, 1985), the root was a frequent Sunday supper dish here in the thirties and forties. Did the prosperity of the following decades have something to do with the unglamorous root's decline?

Celeriac's perfection is best experienced when it is eaten raw; its chewy crunch and assertive flavor are easy crowd-pleasers. It needs no more than thin slicing or grating, and gentle sprinkling with a vinaigrette or creamy piquant dressing. Marinate the absorbent vegetable for several hours or overnight. Cooking mellows its dominant flavor. You can braise or blanch the sliced vegetable to diminish the celery aspect but retain its delicacy before seasoning it. Slices will cook in about 10 to 15 minutes. Do not overcook to mushy blandness.

In northern and Mediterranean Europe, the robust vegetable adds new dimensions to soups and stews, particularly with other root vegetables, such as turnips, parsnips, and carrots. The cooked celeriac can also be pureed and finished with cream or butter and seasonings. With potatoes this is an especially tasty treatment. Try substituting celeriac for its common celery relative in Thanksgiving stuffings. The aromatic flavor goes well with lamb, beef, or duck and other game meat.

Celeriac is a fall and winter vegetable. The root should feel firm, not spongy, and be heavy for its size. Choose medium-size roots, weighing about ¾ pound to 1 pound. The irregular root tendrils, clinging earth, and pungent aroma are normal, healthy aspects. There may or may not be a clump of leaves at the collar. The smoother roots simply have the advantage of being easier to clean and peel. Store celeriac for up to two weeks, or longer if it looks good, in plastic in the vegetable crisper of the refrigerator.

Scrub its bulbous body under running water, remove the scruffy skin with a sharp paring knife, and wash again. The innermost woody section may be too fibrous to use. The cream-colored flesh browns quickly upon exposure to air, so place the peeled vegetable in salted water or in water acidulated with lemon juice or vinegar

(1 tablespoon of lemon juice or vinegar for each cup of water) until you're ready to use it.

As a celery-related plant, it has been known for its diuretic herbal qualities, having been considered useful to those with kidney stones and arthritic conditions. But you may put more stock in its other health advantages. It has modest amounts of iron, calcium, and B vitamins.

Celeriac and Carrot with Mustard Cream Dressing

 *4 servings*

This variation on the classic French appetizer is a good way to introduce anyone to this tasty vegetable.

½ cup heavy cream
¼ cup low-fat yogurt
1 tablespoon chopped sweet pickles
1 tablespoon drained capers
1 tablespoon Dijon mustard
1 tablespoon chopped parsley
⅛ teaspoon cayenne pepper
2 medium-size celeriacs, about 1½ pounds
1 small carrot
Romaine lettuce leaves

1. Beat cream just until it is frothy and almost ready to form peaks. Combine with yogurt, pickles, capers, mustard, parsley, and cayenne.

2. Peel celeriac and carrot. Slice into thin julienne strips by hand or with food processor. Toss with dressing and chill for one hour. Arrange on a bed of romaine lettuce and serve.

Chayote

The chayote is a most unusual squash, introduced to our country by newcomers of Asian descent. Its name derives from *chayotli*, from the Nahuatl language of the Aztecs. West Indians call the mild-flavored vegetable *christophine* after Christopher Columbus.

The chayote is a rambling vine that produces male and female fruit. The female, furrowed with a cleavagelike ridge, is the more preferable, with the smooth male version being less fleshy. The plant has several edible parts, including tuberous roots that are rich in starch, and leaves and shoots that are often added to soups and stews. These components seldom appear in the market.

It is the pale green fruit that tests the cook's imagination. Spines that cover the fruit are usually removed prior to shipment. The fiber-free flesh, unlike that of other squash, retains its crisp texture after cooking. The firm crunchy interior is white and not unlike that of a juicy apple. The vegetable has a high water content— about 90 percent. It is good alone, in which case it needs to be accented with deft seasoning, or with other vegetables.

You can prepare chayote as you would zucchini and any other summer squash—slice and sauté, boil, or steam it, add to casseroles, soups, and stews (more for its texture than its wallflower flavor), stuff it, or add it to Oriental stir-fries. Chayote is a subtly flavored vegetable that works well with most seasonings, especially those of dominant character, such as tomatoes, oregano, chilies, sweet peppers, garlic, curries, and the like. Blanched, it can be added to salads, a crudité tray, or enlivened with a zip of lime juice and sprinkle of salt. It's much better cooked than raw. Its cooking time is slightly longer than other similar squash; it takes about 20 to 25 minutes of sautéing or steaming.

Chayote is a favorite with the Cajun cooks of Louisiana, who know it as *mirliton*. In Mexico and the West Indies, where the vegetable is a popular staple, it may be incorporated into sweet dishes, pureed like pumpkin, or sliced like apples. It appears as a spiced sweet stuffing in peppers in Mexico.

The vegetable has a single seed about the size of a peach pit. The seed cooks to an edible texture faintly reminiscent of pistachios or soy nuts. Remove the seed and stuff the halved chayote with cheese, seasoned chopped beef, or cooked rice and lentils. Due to its high water content, chayote is low in calories.

Chayote can weigh up to 2 pounds, but the ideal size is smaller, about 6 ounces. It is common in Chinese markets; I have never failed to find the vegetable in the stalls of the Asian sellers at Philadelphia's expansive Reading Terminal. Chayotes are available almost all year round. Look for small pale green ones that are firm and blemish-free. Larger ones are good for stuffing. Chayotes store well—up to three months in the refrigerator—but do not allow them to sprout.

Home-Fried Chayote with Rosemary

 *4 servings*

Serve this dish as a low-starch alternative to fried potatoes.

2 large chayotes, peeled and thinly sliced
2 tablespoons butter
2 tablespoons olive oil
3 tablespoons finely minced shallots
2 tablespoons finely minced green pepper
2 teaspoons crushed fresh rosemary leaves
3 tablespoons white wine
1/4 teaspoon salt
Freshly ground black pepper

1. Cook chayote in boiling water for 5 minutes. Drain and set aside.

2. Heat butter and oil, and add shallots and green pepper. Cook 3 minutes. Add chayote and rosemary, stir, and cook another 7 minutes. Add wine and salt and pepper. Cook another 3 minutes and serve.

Chinese Cabbage (including Bok Choy)

The Chinese cabbages are even more confusing to identify than the chicory and endive crew. There are a multitude of the variously straight or curly-leaf heads collectively called Chinese cabbage. With several head shapes—some open and unfurled, others all leaf and stalk, and others tightly wrapped in overlapping sheaths— they vary from dark green to chartreuse, from smooth to frilly, from tenderly sweet to bitter and radishy.

They sport a legion of names too, including Chinese celery cabbage, Napa cabbage, Michili, Peking cabbage, and bok choy (see below), and, to the botanist, brassicas, crucifers, and mustard cabbages. They are all native to eastern Asia and very similar in origin, history, and cultivation. As they are ancient plants of unknown ancestry, the confusion is easily understood.

The two most commonly found Chinese cabbages in the United States are the tall and slender Michili and the short and stout Napa, both very similar with barely perceptible differences. Both have tight wraparound leaves with crinkled edges. Michili is cylindrical and a bit stronger-flavored than Napa. Napa, slightly wrinkly and more barrel-shaped, is usually more easily found.

The Chinese cabbages are finer in taste than our head cabbage, more delicate, and do not wreak the digestive havoc of the more sulfuric species. They do contain a volatile mustard oil, which adds the hint of horseradish piquancy you taste in varying degrees.

Chinese cabbages are cool-weather crops that grow quickly. You'll find them year round. Feel for a densely packed, heavy head (weighing up to 4 pounds), with pale lime-green outer leaves. The inner leaves, like hearts of lettuce, turn to white ribs and are delicately sweeter. The Chinese cabbages store extremely well in the refrigerator for up to two or three weeks. When using, remove tough or damaged outer leaves.

Use versatile Chinese cabbage in every way imaginable. For its vitamin A, potassium, and folic acid, add it raw to salads, or cook it in soups, stir-fry it with tofu, other vegetables, or meat. It cooks quickly—in a matter of minutes—and heating will dissipate any overly emphatic cabbage flavor. Koreans pickle this cabbage into *kimchee*, a refreshingly spicy and piquant condiment also served as a side dish.

Braise, blanch, or stuff the whole leaves, or cream them and prepare au gratin. They absorb flavors readily. This mild cabbage is a perfect bed for poached fish, tofu, or egg dishes. Slice the cabbage across the ribs, or shred, steam, or boil and toss with butter.

Bok choy or *pak choy*, a relative of the cabbage clan, has been available for quite a few years now. The Chinese celery cabbages are believed to be offspring of this variety, which may have bred with a turnip in ancient times. The familiar bok choy has very dark evergreen leaves, with pearly-white, crisp, succulent midribs rising from a bulbous basal stalk. The stalks are smooth, sweet, and mild, with slight hints of cabbage and mustard. Bok choy is commonly stir-fried with shredded pork, a standard addition to wonton soup. Though seldom served raw, its pronounced pepperiness is fine with soy sauce that way.

Tomato-Braised Chinese Cabbage and Ham

 *4 servings*

2 tablespoons vegetable oil
1 onion, chopped
1 cup tomato puree
4 cups meat or vegetable stock
6 cups chopped Chinese cabbage
2 ounces smoked ham, cut into ½-inch cubes
2 teaspoons caraway seeds
¼ teaspoon salt
¼ teaspoon black pepper

Heat oil, add onion, and cook until soft, about 5 minutes. Stir in puree and stock and heat just to boiling. Add cabbage, ham, caraway, salt, and pepper and lower heat to simmer. Cook 15 minutes, stirring occasionally. Serve with noodles or rice.

Collards

Nutritionists, ever in search of more efficient, economical ways to improve the world's diet, might take a good look at collards. For a fifty-cent package of seeds early this spring, my garden has been furnishing me with fresh greens daily. I can't seem to exhaust the prodigious loose-leafed blue-green rosette of each plant that regenerates over and over. With a mother lode of nutrition, the hardy green contains scads more vitamin A than cabbage or broccoli, as much vitamin C in a one-cup serving as in an orange, and almost as much calcium as a half cup of milk, not to mention good amounts of other minerals, namely iron, potassium, and zinc—all especially important to active people.

Similar to kale, except for their unwrinkled leaves, collards are a less renowned member of the cabbage family, with their roots in prehistoric times. Collards made their way to the New World in the seventeenth century with the slaves and have their grandest stature in the repertoire of hearty and homey southern cooking.

Collards have large flat green leaves, and a taste with the peppery aspects of cabbage but a smokier flavor traditionally coaxed along by slow cooking with ham or salt pork, a dish affectionately labeled "a mess of greens."

Select young bunches of collards, with leaves the color of a blue spruce pine, with smooth, matte finish and little leaf damage. Avoid yellowing, limp-leafed heads. Available year round, collards are at peak flavor during the cool months, when the brisker temperatures have allowed them to sweeten. Collards store well for about five to seven days, but, as with all fresh produce, nutrient content diminishes in storage, so do cook these storehouses of nourishment as soon as possible. Store as you would other greens (see page 54). Like most cabbages, they require only casual rinsing to clean.

For years I treated collards Italian-style—steamed, chopped, and sautéed in garlic and olive oil—before I tasted the forcefully hearty, pungent "mess of greens" at a picnic. I like both ways, but find my way easier and perhaps more nutritious. You can cook collards to oblivion as is done for the "mess," and still retain flavor and some soft texture. I prefer to steam the greens (often with Swiss chard, also from my garden) in a Chinese bamboo steamer (a metal basket will do), and then submit them to all manner of guise: cold with a splash of vinaigrette, sautéed with other vegetables, with eggs, or plain with a dash of soy. I've successfully added collards to pasta dishes and enhanced their cabbage flavor with sweet tomato sauce (remember that the vitamin C content of tomatoes can enhance your body's uptake of the iron in greens such as collards).

I liked the underrated vegetable so well when I discovered it a few years ago that I elevated it from its lowly status by adding it to a deliciously seductive cheesecake, savory with onions and dill (recipe follows). Try cooked collards instead of spinach in omelets and frittatas too for a pleasant textural and taste change. Their extroverted flavor is not easily camouflaged, but it is almost always companionable with other assertive tastes—curries, chilies, and Mediterranean spices, to name a few.

Dill-Onion-Collard Cheesecake

 *8 to 10 servings*

This keeps its savoriness for days. It's good at room temperature or you can reheat it by the slice in the oven. If you don't have whole-grain bread handy for the crust, add some ground walnuts for more flavor.

Crust
2 tablespoons melted butter or oil
1 cup whole-grain bread crumbs

Filling
1 bunch (about 1 to 1½ pounds) collards
2 tablespoons butter
2 tablespoons vegetable oil
1 large white onion, chopped
5 eggs
2 pounds cottage (or ricotta) cheese
3 tablespoons chopped fresh dill, or 2 teaspoons dried
½ teaspoon salt
¼ teaspoon black pepper

1. *Prepare crust:* Preheat oven to 350°F. Melt butter in a 10-inch springform pan in the oven. Stir in bread crumbs and mix well. Remove about ¼ cup of the bread crumbs and set aside.

Press remaining mixture into a crust about 1 inch up the sides. Bake for 10 minutes and set aside.

2. *Prepare filling:* Steam collards until tender, about 20 to 25 minutes.

3. Heat butter and oil. Add onion and cook until tender, about 10 minutes. When collards are cool enough to handle, chop coarsely and stir into onion.

4. Combine eggs, cheese, dill, salt, and pepper in a large mixing bowl. Stir in collards and onion and mix well. Pour into crust. Sprinkle top with reserved crumb mixture. Bake for 1 hour. Turn oven off, open door, and allow to cool in oven for at least 1 hour. Cool thoroughly at room temperature before refrigerating or serving.

Daikon

"A giant white radish that looks like a huge albino carrot" is how Jack Murdich describes this greatly oversized Oriental radish in his *Buying Produce* (Hearst Books, 1986). As a root staple in the East that can weigh as much as 2 pounds (up to 50, if the farmer lets it), *daikon* is the Japanese appellation. The Chinese call it *lo-pak* or *loh-baak.* Called *mooli* in India and Africa, botanists say it is a centuries-old cultivation of the round red radish. All the radishes belong to the same crucifer or mustard family.

The daikon is big and crisp, juicy, mild to sharp, with surprising punch. It is edible raw or cooked. All you need do to prepare it is wash, peel the outer skin, and slice into wafers.

Although once only Chinese markets carried the exotic radish, it now abounds at many produce stands. Look for a crisp, not rubbery, vegetable, with a juicy clarity, no dull or grayish tint. The root should be heavy, solid, and unblemished, with the pungent smell of radish. Generally the daikon is marketed without its green tops. It is not nearly so perishable as the smaller white or red salad radishes.

Slice, dice, or chop daikon and perk up any raw vegetable mélange or salad with it. In Japanese cuisine the cream-colored vegetable is popular grated and seasoned or shredded and spiced with ginger, garlic, soy, and lime and served with broiled or poached fatty fish, such as tuna, mackerel, and salmon. Add daikon disks to soups, stews, or stir-fries. Spike a yogurt or sour cream dressing or dip with its peppery surprise or make a sweet-sour relish condiment.

Daikon Vegetable Salad with Oriental Dressing

 *4 servings*

Dressing
1/3 cup peanut oil
1/2 teaspoon sesame oil
1/3 cup brown rice vinegar (or cider vinegar)
2 tablespoons light soy sauce
1 tablespoon toasted sesame seeds
1 teaspoon mirin (sweet rice wine—see page 224)
1 teaspoon grated ginger
1/2 teaspoon finely minced garlic
1 teaspoon fresh lime juice

Salad
2 cups coarsely shredded daikon
3 carrots, peeled and shredded
1 small red pepper, very thinly sliced
1 stalk celery, very thinly sliced

1. *Prepare dressing*: Combine all ingredients in a bowl and mix well.
2. *Prepare salad*: Toss ingredients in with dressing to coat well. Chill at least 1 hour before serving.

Dandelion

This bitter green is the same rogue that taunts the keeper of suburban lawns. The French name, *dent de lion*, means "lion's tooth," no doubt referring to its jagged leaves, which somewhat resemble curly endive but are less fleshy. It is Italian and French cooking, along with some American Deep South dwellers, who give the humble weed its culinary due. I have also seen the green sold frequently by the Pennsylvania Dutch merchants in the big farmer's market in Allentown, Pennsylvania.

Although Europeans and Asians have eaten it for centuries, dandelion does seem to thrive with little help just about anywhere. Cooks aren't the only ones who acknowledge the dandelion's worth. Herbalists tout its healing ability. It is considered beneficial to liver ailments, with laxative and digestive-aiding properties. Winemakers are fond of the heart-warming brew its flowers render.

Use dandelion (greens only) raw or cooked. Add the feisty green to salads along with a mix of other bitter and sweet greens, such as arugula, watercress, escarole, lamb's quarters (a "new" salad bowl green discussed on page 105). Use dandelion in wilted salads, with hot dressings; this is popular in France and Italy. Boil or steam the green, then season with oil or butter, salt, and pepper. Since it can be astringently bitter, it may be a good idea to mix the vitamin-A- and -C-rich green (calcium, iron, and potassium are among its mineral content) with others, such as collards, chard, kale, and mustard greens, for a better balance of flavor. Substitute dandelion for some of the spinach in omelets or quiche.

When selecting dandelion in the market, choose the smaller-leafed heads, as they are the least bitter and most tender. The greens are best in early spring. Look for springy, crisp heads that are not wilted, limp, or marred by many brown spots. When picking this hardy green "in the wild," make sure you pick only those you know have not been sprayed or tainted. Store as you would other greens (see page 54), and use within a few days. Rinse well to remove dirt, especially at the base of the head. Drain or spin dry if using in salad, otherwise proceed with cooking.

Dandelion with Creamy Lemon Poppy Seed Dressing

 4 servings

½ cup olive oil
1 egg yolk
2 tablespoons fresh lemon juice
1 tablespoon poppy seeds
2 teaspoons Dijon-style mustard
1 teaspoon minced fresh tarragon, or ½ teaspoon dried
1 teaspoon sugar
¼ teaspoon salt
⅛ teaspoon white pepper
1 head (about 1 pound) small-leafed dandelion, cleaned and dried
8 beet slices
½ cup walnut pieces
¼ cup chopped scallions

1. Combine oil, egg, juice, seeds, mustard, tarragon, sugar, salt, and pepper in a jar with a lid. Shake well, until ingredients are combined well.

2. Break dandelion into bite-size pieces and divide among 4 salad plates. Divide beets, walnuts, and scallions over salads. Just before serving, pour dressing over each salad.

Elephant Garlic

This jumbo-size version of true garlic (*Allium sativum*) is perhaps meant for that half of the world who would like to join those of us who don't shrink from the stinking rose. What a promise for those who have aversions to the lingering perfume—garlic flavor that is mild and with none of the highly dreaded aftereffects.

Elephant cloves (*Allium scorodoprasum*), which are roughly the size of a quail egg, slip right out of their papery skin, another benefit of this wondrous spice. In theory, one clove of the big stuff is equal to about eighteen to twenty cloves of the normal-size garlic, shaving minutes off prep time. Some connoisseurs feel that this pachyderm of a spice hasn't been around long enough to prove its virtues. However, it is definitely the more soft-hearted of the two species, providing essence and mild taste, but not the long-lived garlic pungency. If you like nip but not sting (some may say *stink*), this garlic's for you.

Though it has more bark than bite, the elephant garlic still possesses allicin, the volatile oil that lends garlic its spirit. Allicin is also responsible for the legendary health powers of garlic, including its antibiotic, antifungal, and most recently, its blood-toning or anti-blood-clotting effects (of interest to those with heart disease).

This macro herb can be a mini side dish in itself, steamed or boiled as a vegetable, then served with a cream or cheese sauce. And, of course, you can substitute it for true garlic in any dish. You can add thin raw slices to salads, for the similar but less imposing effect of a few scallion rings.

I've yet to see presses for elephant garlic, so if you wish to crush a toe (foot sounds more apt) of the overgrown spice, you must first slice it; or simply mash the shallot-sized clove on a cutting board with a knife handle or other heavy blunt object. Store elephant garlic as you would regular garlic—at room temperature, away from light and moisture, never in the refrigerator; or submerge the whole cloves in oil, to which they will readily impart their controversial essence.

Elephant Garlic, Tomato, and Basil Frittata

 *4 servings*

In addition to its mild flavor, the garlic imparts its crunchy texture to this dish.

2 tablespoons oil or butter
4 to 6 cloves elephant garlic (or more, if desired), thinly sliced
1 large, very ripe tomato, chopped
¼ cup chopped fresh basil, or 2 teaspoons dried
½ teaspoon dried oregano
¼ teaspoon crushed red pepper
4 eggs
¼ cup grated Parmesan
½ cup grated fontina or Swiss cheese

1. Heat oil or butter. Add garlic and sauté until lightly golden, about 5 minutes. Add tomato and cook until disintegrated, about 5 minutes. Stir in basil, oregano, and pepper and remove from heat.

2. Combine eggs and cheeses in a large bowl. Mix well. Scrape tomato mixture into eggs and mix well. Wipe out pan and grease lightly again, then heat. Pour in egg mixture and cook over moderate heat. When bottom is set, in about 3 minutes, start lifting sides with a spatula so that uncooked mixture seeps under. To make sure frittata is cooked through, cover pan during last minute or two of cooking to steam-cook. Slice into wedges and serve.

Escarole

Escarole is a bitter leafy green, yet another of those longtime backseat Italian vegetables coming out of oblivion in this country. The earthy green holds special memories of a comforting stew for me. Called *scarola* (Italian for "escarole") in my family, this old winter standard consisted of a thin broth of the boiled green with red kidney beans and spicy Italian meatballs. The meat-stretching recipe was perfect for a big family such as ours and packed an enormous amount of iron. My parents have tampered with the traditional recipe with good results, evolving an updated variation using ground fennel seeds and onions, which I share here.

In his book *Produce* (Friendly Press, 1984), Bruce Beck explains, "Science has decided that all the chicories and endives are botanically *chicorium*, but popular usage has confused the issue greatly. Names vary not just from country to country, but regionally as well." I refer you to him for the "cold facts." In this book I discuss escarole, Belgian endive (page 60), and radicchio (page 119)— all called chicory in one land or another—as distinct entities.

Escarole is a flat-leafed cousin of curly chicory (or curly endive, depending where you live). Escarole's leaves are fleshier, greener, flatter, while those of curly chicory are narrow and spinier with curly serrated edges. Escarole belongs to the species *Cichorium endivia* and chicory to *Cichorium intybus*. Both are believed to be native to India. Both types have a lighter yellow inner heart that is due to a blanching method in the fields where the greens are grown. Both escarole and curly endive are used raw in salads, generally with other types of lettuce, or cooked as a vegetable. I have used both in the preparations described above, but find the thicker escarole to taste more authentic. The curly endive is slightly more bitter, but both can be tough if not cooked long enough.

In the market escarole, a winter vegetable, looks like a head of disorganized lettuce. Choose crisp and fresh-looking, not wilted or limp, heads. Store and clean escarole as you would all greens (see page 54).

Besides being simply steamed, boiled, or sautéed in garlicky olive oil, escarole works well in salads with a creamy vinaigrette to foil its bitterness. It may appear in the Provençale favorite *salade niçoise*, or with a hot bacon and crouton dressing. Braised and mixed with a creamy nutmeg-scented béchamel is also a good treatment. The bitter principle makes escarole a digestive aid that those of Mediterranean descent seem ever fond of, especially against common gastrointestinal complaints. And don't forget this leafy green's notable iron and vitamin C content.

Escarole and Beans

 *4 servings*

This is my parents' variation on the hearty peasant Italian classic *Scarola e Fagioli*. Although you can use already-ground fennel seed, we prefer to grind our own in a spice or coffee grinder as we make the dish. Serve with sausage or Italian meatballs.

2 tablespoons olive oil
1 large onion, chopped
1 large head (about 1½ pounds) of escarole, cleaned
1 teaspoon ground fennel seeds
2 cups cooked red kidney beans (adjust salt if using canned)
Salt and pepper to taste

Heat oil in a large pot. Add onion and cook until browned, about 10 minutes. Add escarole, fennel, and 1 cup of water. Cover pot and steam, stirring occasionally, until escarole is tender, about 20 minutes. Add more water if necessary. Stir in beans and cook just until heated through. Season to taste. If serving with meatballs or sausage, cook the meat separately and add to escarole with beans.

Fennel

Fennel is a sweet, licorice-flavored vegetable steeped in herbal lore and tradition. Besides its long-standing appeal to Mediterranean cooks, it has, throughout the ages, been considered an antidote for numerous ailments—from coughs, colic, and abdominal cramps to evil and obesity.

There are two types of edible fennel, commonly called *anise*, both imparting the characteristic scent and flavor to varying degrees. *Common* or *wild fennel* is grown for its seeds and leaves. The seeds, a popular seasoning for Italian sausage, may also flavor cookies, breads, and other baked goods. The feathery leaves can be brewed into a calming tea. Used either fresh or dried, they mate famously with fish dishes—especially soups, stews, and sauces. Fennel leaves help lessen the oiliness of fish such as salmon or mackerel. If you're ever in a seafood restaurant along the Mediterranean perhaps you'll experience the same delightful use for dried fennel twigs that I once did. Before my very eyes the waiter ignited the stalky pile of small branches, deftly flambéing my grilled fish until it was perfectly smoked and redolent of fennel.

It is the second type of fennel, *Florence fennel* or *sweet fennel*, that I find most versatile. Florence fennel—often called *finocchio* by Italian cooks—resembles squat celery with thick overlapping basal stalks. Most abundant in fall and winter, it can be found in large produce markets in most cosmopolitan areas.

The humble appearance of Florence fennel does not indicate its culinary worth. Its mild licorice flavor adds a new and refreshing dimension to raw vegetable salads (cut away the darker green woody stalks), but there are many ways to enjoy cooked fennel. Braising in stock or a seasoned liquid brings out fennel's unique flavor. Sautéing in butter with a simple fresh herb also points up its pleasant taste; sage, sweet basil, marjoram, and tarragon all mingle nicely with fennel. Fennel's crisp sweetness is a wonderful foil for robust Italian cheeses; pair it with a Gorgonzola and ricotta mixture or bake tender stalks of fennel stuffed with grated Parmesan, Romano, or Pecorino and bread crumbs. Steamed or parboiled fennel goes well with a light cream sauce, and it can be pureed as a soup or sauce base by itself. Crunchy fennel can also be paired with tomatoes, lentils, rice, and potatoes, and even used in desserts. Look for firm, crisp-looking bulbs of fennel without too much browning or signs of drying. The top woody stalks may have been trimmed (a good thing if you're paying by the pound) but some of the dark green lacy foliage should be intact. Store fennel in the vegetable crisper and use within a few days to enjoy the licorice flavor at its best.

Sautéed Veal with Fennel and Red Peppers
Vitello all'uccelletto

 *4 to 6 servings*

This is a variation on a recipe I developed for *Attenzione* magazine, November 1984.

3 tablespoons olive oil
2 pounds veal shoulder, cut into 1-inch cubes
2 tablespoons butter
1 small fennel bulb (about 6 ounces), thinly sliced
1 medium-size red pepper, thinly sliced
¼ cup dry white wine
1½ teaspoons fresh thyme, or ½ teaspoon dried
Salt and pepper to taste

1. Heat oil in a large skillet. Brown veal cubes over moderately high heat until cooked through. Remove from skillet and set aside.

2. Heat butter in skillet. Add fennel and red peppers and cook over moderate heat for 10 minutes.

3. Stir in wine and thyme and cook over moderate heat until liquid is reduced by half, about 7 minutes. Stir in veal and cook just until meat is heated through. Season to taste and serve.

Fiddlehead Ferns

Cozy coils, kinetically poised, fiddleheads look like something about to slither across the produce counter. But the plumed lush green swirls are really inanimate shoots that have been plucked in their prime before they advance to a less gastronomically significant stage. For fiddlehead describes not a specific species of fern, but rather an early stage of development of any fern, in the process of "circinate vernation." What this fancy term means simply is that the ferns progress from their tightly curled embryo posture to a more open airy spiral. What we of connoisseur foraging want is the opening shoot that appears like the scroll end of a violin, whence this comestible's name.

The shoots of the ostrich fern, *Matteuccia struthiopteris*, so named because it resembles the head and neck of that bird, are the ones most commonly available to us commercially. The springy fronds slice through the soil from April through July. The ferns thrive in the damp, moist area near streams or in woods, in New England, Canada, and much of eastern North America, and command a rather high price for their woodsy succulence.

As a dear gourmet item, fiddlehead ferns are pretty much the province of specialty-food markets—up there with cardoons and fresh morels. Look for sprightly appearance in the moist, springily curled fronds. About 1 to 1½ inches in diameter, with minimal tail, is a good size. Much larger, and the fern will be a mouthful of green wood and fiber. Wash them gingerly under cold water and dry with paper towel just before cooking.

The blush is on the rose a fleeting moment, so to speak, with these curlicues, so don't store them very long. Cook them the day you buy them, in fact, for top freshness. Wrap them in paper towel and plastic and refrigerate until you are ready for them.

Use fiddleheads fresh as a cold salad appetizer or sautéed, boiled, or steamed as a delicate green vegetable like asparagus. Cream sauces or simple vinaigrettes of lemon or mustard charm forth the fern's asparagus-mushroom aspects. Hollandaise or flavored mayonnaise points up the earthy herby flavor of the emerald coils. Several cookbooks suggest the orange-scented Maltaise sauce. The green's nutty flavor, which reminds me of sweet wheatgrass, can also be enhanced with melted butter for a simple delicious appetizer.

Fiddlehead Ferns and Porcini with Cream

 *4 servings*

1 ounce (about 1½ cups) dried porcini mushrooms
1 pound fiddlehead ferns
2 tablespoons unsalted butter
1 tablespoon minced shallots
1 cup heavy cream
Salt and freshly ground black pepper

1. Place mushrooms in a small bowl and cover with warm water to reconstitute for at least 20 minutes.
2. Meanwhile, cut off any tough stem base of ferns. Remove

any brown spots and rinse. Drop into boiling water and cook for 5 minutes. Drain immediately.

3. Drain porcini, reserving liquid. Make sure they are free of all grit, rinsing under water, if necessary. Chop on cutting board into small (about ½-inch) pieces.

4. Melt butter over moderate heat in a large skillet. Add shallots and porcini and cook 5 minutes, until shallots are soft. Stir in cream and ½ cup well-strained porcini liquid. Cook over low heat until thickened, about 5 minutes.

5. Add ferns to cream and cook just until heated through. Season to taste and turn into serving dish.

Jerusalem Artichokes

Despite its name, the Jerusalem artichoke (or *sunchoke*) is a native of North America and is the knobbed stem-tuber of a sunflower. *Jerusalem* is the corruption of the Italian word for sunflower, *girasole*. The juicy, crisp tubers have translucent white flesh covered with papery walnut-brown skin and look very much like stout fresh ginger. Succulent and crisp, they are sweet, nutty, and do have the delicacy of artichoke hearts. They have been compared to water chestnuts and jicama, but have much more complexity of flavor than these. If you have tasted only bland ones, it may be because they have been harvested too early in the fall, before the frost. Having lived some time in Pennsylvania Dutch country, I have sampled the local farmers' chokes right at their peak of perfection and can vouch for their potential for full intensity of taste.

An interesting nutritional note is made about the Jerusalem artichoke in Rodale's *The Organic Gardener's Complete Guide to Vegetables and Fruits* (1982). The sunchoke apparently is a unique tuber with no starch content, as it stores its carbohydrate as a substance called *inulin*, found in the roots and sap of some plants. This makes it a good potato substitute for diabetics whose condition allows only the most judicious use of starch foods. The artichoke is also low in calories and high in vitamin B_1, potassium, and other minerals. If you've ever sampled low-starch artichoke pasta, usually available in natural-foods stores, you may not have realized that this vegetable, not the globe artichoke, was its foundation.

The knobby vegetable is difficult to peel, though boiling helps it slip right out of its skin. The exposed raw vegetable discolors quickly, so as you peel and slice, place it in acidulated water (about 1 tablespoon of lemon juice or vinegar for every cup of water needed to cover the slices). Boiled sunchokes are often pureed with cream and butter and sometimes with potato for a sweet and earthy flavor contrast. The vegetable's sweetness invites onion, cream, and dashes of clove, cinnamon, or nutmeg. But Mediterranean cooks also season it with tomatoes and garlic. Its gnarly fingers can be peeled, sliced, and sautéed with sweet butter, garnished with parsley, dill, or chives, or dipped in batter and deep-fried. Sunchokes can be eaten raw—grated or sliced into a salad. Cover the exposed raw flesh immediately with an acidic dressing. Chopped and added to potato salads, Jerusalem artichokes cut the calorie count way down while adding crunch and taste. Fresh herbs such as basil, tarragon, and mint enhance its artichoke likeness.

Select firm Jerusalem artichokes that are not mushy or watery. The earthy tan skin is naturally mottled-looking, but should not be blemished through to the flesh. Store Jerusalem artichokes in the refrigerator. You can keep them for up to two weeks, but their peak flavor may diminish in storage.

Jerusalem Artichokes au Gratin

 *4 to 6 servings*

8 medium-size Jerusalem artichokes
3 tablespoons butter
2 tablespoons flour
²/₃ cup meat or vegetable stock
²/₃ cup milk
2 ounces grated Parmesan
2 ounces grated Swiss cheese
¼ cup bread crumbs
1 tablespoon melted butter

1. Scrub artichokes clean. Steam until tender, about 30 minutes. Cool, peel, and cube. Place in a buttered 1½-quart casserole.
2. Melt 3 tablespoons butter in a heavy saucepan. Stir in flour and cook for 2 minutes. Very slowly add stock and milk, stirring constantly to avoid lumping. Cook until thick and smooth, about 10 minutes. Add cheese and cook until melted.
3. Preheat oven to 350°F. Pour sauce over artichokes. Mix bread crumbs with melted butter and sprinkle over top of casserole. Bake for 15 minutes, or until top is lightly golden.

Jicama

I first encountered the root vegetable jicama (pronounced hee-CA-ma) in the colorful streets of the Mexican fishing village San Blas. Every day about noontime, I'd find the same street vendor and watch the brown hands smear salt, a smidgeon of chili pepper, and a generous squeeze of fresh lime juice on the thick white slab of jicama. The juicy tuber was not only a low-calorie light refreshment perfect for the tropical climate, but an orgy of water, starch, and sweetness so satisfying to my palate and filling to my stomach that I craved nothing else until the sumptuous seafood at dinner.

Back in the States I searched for this tasty vegetable and found it in the fresh produce markets of San Francisco's Chinatown. Although its name is Spanish, meaning "edible storage root," both Mexican and Chinese cuisine have applications for this tuber. Some describe jicama's taste as similar to that of water chestnuts with a slight hint of sweetness. It can easily stand in for them in Chinese dishes.

The sight of the whole brownish knotty root brings to mind coconuts, potatoes, and misshapen turnips. It has a very tough and thick outer skin that you can peel off easily with a paring knife or rotary blade, revealing the sweet white flesh beneath. The roots range in weight from 1 to 6 pounds and from 3 to 6 inches in diameter. A good rule of thumb is, the smaller the juicier. The delicate taste is best appreciated in the raw state, but you can also prepare jicama as you would sweet potatoes. Chop, slice, or dice it and add to Chinese dishes with other vegetables. It has a pleasing crunchy texture, which it retains even after cooking.

Jicama's sweetness blends nicely with the flavor of soy sauce. Steeping slices of jicama in seasoned marinades makes this low-starch, low-calorie vegetable a perfect munchy food. It contains quantities of vitamins A, B complex, and C, along with calcium and phosphorus. Party dips, cottage cheese, fruit or vegetable salad—all become less trite served with fresh jicama slices.

South Americans differentiate between *jicama de agua* and *jicama de leche*. The first displays clear juice when bruised, the second a milky liquid. You are most apt to find the former in this country's Mexican or Chinese produce markets. Store jicama in your refrigerator's vegetable bin and use within seven to ten days.

Jicama-Spinach Salad or Appetizer

 6 *to* 8 *servings*

1 10½-ounce package frozen chopped spinach
1½ cups grated jicama
½ cup chopped scallions
3 tablespoons minced celery
½ cup plain yogurt
¼ cup sour cream
¼ cup mayonnaise
1 teaspoon Dijon mustard
1 tablespoon fresh lemon juice
¼ teaspoon salt
⅛ teaspoon cayenne pepper
1 tablespoon chopped fresh cilantro (optional)

Completely thaw spinach and drain well. Combine all ingredients in a large mixing bowl and let stand at room temperature for one hour. Serve as a cold buffet salad or as an appetizer dip, with bread, crackers, or chips.

Kabocha Squash

Kabocha is a squat, mottled pine-green squash, with attributes similar to those of buttercup squash, a turban-shaped variety. Kabocha weighs about 3 to 5 pounds, and is mostly prized for its creamy-smooth fiber-free flesh. The pulp is sweet and puddinglike but blander than other squash varieties and presently most appreciated by Japanese cooks. Several slightly differing varieties of squash may be called kabocha.

Look for kabocha in Japanese food markets. Choose firm, heavy vegetables free of soft or decaying spots or stems. Store like other squash at room temperature for up to three or four weeks.

Use kabocha as you would any of the winter squash variety— simply baked with butter and a touch of brown sugar or maple syrup, or boiled and seasoned (remove the clump of central seeds and fiber). Mash or puree it and season as you would mashed potatoes. Bake it like an apple with maple syrup and walnuts. You can also turn it into a fine, rich-textured (high starch) dessert, such as pudding, pie filling, or quick bread. Use as you would pumpkin puree.

Kabocha with Lime-Coriander Sauce

 *4 servings*

This simple side dish (or snack) contrasts the sweet flesh of the squash with the sharp citrusy notes of the sauce.

2 medium-size kabocha squash (about 4 to 5 pounds)
½ cup (1 stick) unsalted butter
4 teaspoons fresh lime juice
½ teaspoon ground coriander
¼ teaspoon white pepper
¼ teaspoon sugar
1 tablespoon minced fresh cilantro (coriander leaves)

1. Preheat oven to 350°F. Place squash on a baking sheet and bake for about 45 to 60 minutes, until skin is easily pierced with a fork or knife.

2. Meanwhile, prepare sauce. Melt butter over low heat in a

heavy saucepan. Stir in remaining ingredients and remove from heat.

3. Slice slightly cooled squash in half. Scrape out seeds. Spoon sauce over each half and serve hot.

Kale

Kale is actually a primitive form of cabbage, related to collards and other leafy Brassicas such as Scotch blue or something called "ornamental kale." The last is a gaudy violet-streaked cabbage (sometimes sold as "salad savoy") with crinkled leaves, best left to its showy function.

Kale is a Scottish word that derives from the Greek and Roman words *coles* and *caulis*, which referred to cabbage family members. Kale has the strident pungency of the cabbages tempered by a pervasive sweetness. There are several varieties of kale with subtle flavor differences and identity based on leaf color and shape. Some are blue, curled, and tall-leafed, while others have smoky-green leaves with more spreading demeanor.

A cool-season crop, kale withstands the most adverse conditions. It is a hale and hardy plant that can weather a brute frost, and even sweetens its yield under one. It keeps providing fresh greens at lean times of the year and helped keep Europeans alive during the dead of standstill winters in olden days. This should be a big selling point for health-minded people today, who know the value of a daily dose of vitamins A and C—both recognized by the National Institutes of Health as potential cancer deterrents. Kale also delivers some B_2 and the ever-important minerals calcium and iron, among others. Kale leads the pack with all of these nutrients.

Kale's frilly blue-green leaves have relegated it to garnish status in most places in the United States outside the South, a role for which this tasty, crisp, nutritious vegetable is highly overqualified. Kale is not bitter as some of its clan can be and its snapping brisk texture cannot be easily cooked to mush. Yet it is a bit too coarse to enjoy raw.

Kale may be treated like collards in the kitchen. Like collards too, it is an earmark of southern cooking. As a boiled green standard, it has a strong flavor often matched with the smokiness of salt pork or bacon. You can add it to soups to change a docile broth into a robust one, or stuff the parboiled leaves as you would cabbage—with ground meat, cooked rice, lentils, or other grains. Kale will give a stir-fry more snap or it can easily stand alone, sautéed and seasoned with lemon juice, salt, and pepper, a cream sauce, or chilled with a vinaigrette. An Irish dish pairs boiled kale with potatoes, carrots, leeks, and cream in a soulfully satisfying blend.

Young leaves deliver the best flavor and texture. Choose spritely crisp, blue-green leaves, not limp yellowing ones. Store kale in the refrigerator like other greens (see page 54) where it will keep well for a long time without wilting.

Kale, Potatoes, and Sausage

 *4 servings*

1 pound Italian sausage
1 large onion, chopped
6 cups chicken stock
½ pound kale, coarsely chopped
¼ teaspoon crushed red pepper
5 medium-size red potatoes, quartered
Salt to taste

1. Cut sausage into 3-inch pieces. Brown in a large soup pot. Add onion during last 5 minutes of browning and stir.

2. Add stock, kale, pepper, and potatoes to pot. Bring to boil, lower heat, and simmer until potatoes are tender, about 20 minutes. Add salt to taste. Serve with large crusty wedges of bread.

Kohlrabi

In his book *Greene on Greens* (Workman, 1984), Bert Greene notes that kohlrabi's ugliness is only skin deep. He also agrees with Alice B. Toklas's assessment that this odd-looking member of the cabbage (Brassica) family has "the pungency of a highborn radish bred to a lowbrow cucumber." While kohlrabi's taste and appearance may challenge the chef's sensibility, the green, white, or purple turnip-size knobs baffle plant historians outright; they cannot agree if prehistoric man, the Romans, or a Renaissance botanist first cultivated the vegetable.

Kohlrabi's name, deriving from the German *Kohl* meaning cabbage, and *Rabi* meaning turnip, provides the cook with the best clue to this summer (June/July) vegetable's culinary possibilities. In fact many cooks find kohlrabi's taste very reminiscent of turnips, and the two vegetables easily interchange in recipes. Along with Chinese cabbage, kohlrabi is the mildest-tasting member of the Brassica clan. Unlike its strong-flavored relatives, kohlrabi does not become sulfurous in cooking.

The bulbous plant stem that grows above ground and the dark spiky leaves that grow up from these knobs are both edible. However, the squat bulbs are more often the star attraction, for the leaves quickly toughen as they mature. If the leaves are newly sprouted, steam them until tender to the touch of a fork and eat them plain or seasoned like other greens.

What to do with the eccentric swollen stem part? Cooked or raw, creamed or plain in soups, casseroles, patties, relishes, slaws, and salads, the bulbs adapt well to both simple and elaborate treatment. A simple preparation is to steam the bulbs (30 to 35 minutes) or boil them (25 to 30 minutes), slice, bathe them in butter, and season to taste. If you prefer something more elaborate, then try the recipe that follows.

Note that you can cook the bulbs with the skin on and then slip it off easily when they are cooled. Or peel the fibrous covering first, as you would a potato.

When buying kohlrabi, feel the bulbs to make sure that they are firm and crisp with no cracks or splits and are no more than 2 to 3 inches in diameter. Any bigger indicates age and therefore toughness. The top greens should be crisp and brightly colored. The greens will keep for two or three days in the refrigerator, and with the leaves removed, the bulbs can be stored at the same temperature for two to three weeks.

Braised Kohlrabi with Caraway

 *4 servings*

2 pounds kohlrabi, trimmed and peeled
2 tablespoons butter
¼ cup beef stock
¼ cup sherry
2 teaspoons caraway seeds
Salt and pepper to taste
Chopped fresh parsley

1. Slice kohlrabi into ¼-inch-thick strips. Heat butter in heavy skillet and add kohlrabi, tossing to coat well.

2. Stir in stock, sherry, and caraway. Cover and simmer until tender, about 12 minutes. Uncover and sauté over high heat for several minutes, until nicely colored. Season to taste with salt and pepper. Garnish with parsley and serve.

Kohlrabi and Ham Patties

 *4 servings*

6 medium-size kohlrabi
¼ pound ham, diced
2 eggs, beaten
¼ cup bread crumbs
2 tablespoons minced green pepper
2 tablespoons minced onion
2 tablespoons chopped fresh parsley
½ teaspoon marjoram
½ teaspoon chervil
¼ teaspoon salt
¼ teaspoon black pepper
3 tablespoons oil

1. Trim, peel, and shred kohlrabi. Add to boiling water and simmer, covered, for 15 minutes. Drain and cool.

2. Combine remaining ingredients except oil in a bowl. Stir in kohlrabi. Heat oil in a large skillet. Pour in kohlrabi mixture, and cook over moderate heat until bottom is golden brown. Divide into quarters with spatula and turn each quarter over to brown on other side. Serve hot.

Lamb's Quarters

Lamb's quarters (*Chenopodium album*), not to be confused with the prim sophisticate of salad greenery, lamb's lettuce (also called *mâche*; see page 109), is another green now coming into its own.

The plant grows up to 3 feet in height, with triangular leaves and prodigiously flowering spikes. Its silvery flush has also earned it the name *white goosefoot*.

The foliage, especially the tender young tips, can be eaten either raw or steamed and is more plentiful in calcium and vitamins A and C than its cousin, spinach. The American Indians used the plant's edible seeds ground into a flour for making bread, while herbalists tout the plant's healing properties when used as a poultice for treating soreness and swelling.

You may not find lamb's quarters at your local produce stand, but you'll spot its wedge-shaped leaves in your garden or wherever there are rich soil, manure piles, and compost heaps. If you forage it from the wild, do make sure it's from an area that's not sprayed or too near a roadside that's susceptible to car pollution.

Lamb's Quarters with Cucumber-Dill Dressing

 *4 servings*

1 pound of lamb's quarters, cleaned and drained
½ cucumber, peeled, seeded, and finely chopped
¼ cup sour cream
¼ cup buttermilk
2 tablespoons mayonnaise
1 tablespoon fresh lemon juice
1 teaspoon Dijon mustard
1 teaspoon sugar
2 tablespoons chopped fresh dill
¼ teaspoon salt

1. Steam the lamb's quarters for about 5 minutes, until wilted.
2. Combine the remaining ingredients and stir until blended well. Spoon dressing over individual servings of lamb's quarters.

Lotus Root

Lotus roots, actually the roots of a certain water lily, are a popular ingredient in Asian cooking. Food books invariably describe the lotus root's appearance as a string of fat brown sausages. But what lyricism the East ascribes to this grotesque root and the pristine water lily arising from it: the flower is a sun symbol, its development through its watery element toward light and air a Buddhist parable for the soul's pursuit of nirvana. In China the male organ is seen in the water lily bud and the female one in the open blossom. In India the sexual act is portrayed by the rising and expansion of the flower. The Egyptians and Japanese also view the plant as sacred and mystical, seeing its features in a similar light.

The root's grubby appearance certainly does belie all this metaphysical and ethereal portent! Yet, while we Westerners are busy describing it as sausage links or a tuber with an hourglass shape, the Chinese have been deftly working the rhizome (a subsoil stem) into their cooking.

The root segments of the lotus vary from 5 to 12 inches in length, 2 to 3 inches in diameter. They may appear cleaned or dirt-caked. The skin is thin but tough, a fawn to pinkish color. The mucilaginous flesh varies, too, from buff to rose or salmon-tinted. The young tender roots are mild, delicate, slightly sweet, and possess more crunch than taste, but in an aromatic way.

The subtle nature of lotus root makes it a good partner for strong meats, such as pork or beef. The crisp flesh can be sliced into oval disks, matchstick slivers, or dicelike chunks and stir-fried with beef or, more commonly, braised with pork. The crunchy texture does not dissipate with cooking. The cut-up root can enhance any mixed-vegetable medley or soup, or it can be prepared alone, sautéed and seasoned like sliced potatoes. A cross section of the lotus root reveals a kaleidoscope of cavities running the length. These geometrically shaped hollows lend the sliced pond plant eye-catching artistry in many dishes.

Boiling or steaming cooks sliced lotus root in about 10 to 15 minutes. You can use the root as you would any other starchy vegetables, such as turnips, potatoes, jicama, or water chestnuts. Lotus root slices are a common tempura ingredient. They may also be found in Indian pickles or cooked and mashed into spicy vegetarian meatballs. The vegetable can appear in dishes composed with bean curd, or tofu, another food that is more texture than taste until seasonings enliven it. A festive treat of lotus root, carrots, and winter melon is fashioned into a candied confection during the Chinese New Year.

Look for lotus roots in the summer in stores carrying Chinese produce. They are as hard as a light porous wood. Unfortunately, only inspection of interior flesh will reveal the old from the more desirable young, so find a trustworthy shopkeeper. Select unblemished roots for easiest cleaning.

The roots store well for up to two weeks in the refrigerator. To prepare, scrub away caked dirt, then peel with a knife or potato peeler and slice off the neck ends. As you slice, place the quickly browning flesh in water acidulated with 1 tablespoon of vinegar or lemon juice for every cup of water used.

Stir-Fried Lotus Root

 4 to 6 servings

¾ pound lotus root, peeled and thinly sliced
2 tablespoons peanut oil
1 tablespoon soy sauce
2 teaspoons vinegar
¼ teaspoon sugar
2 tablespoons chopped fresh chives

1. Place lotus root in saucepan, cover with water, and bring to a boil. Simmer for 5 minutes, then drain.

2. Heat wok and add oil. Add lotus root and stir to coat. Cook about 5 minutes, then add soy, vinegar, and sugar and toss for 1 minute longer. Toss into serving dish with chives. Serve hot.

Mâche

Mâche (*Valerianella locusta*), riding the crest of the new wave of salad-bowl greens, is a native plant in much of Europe. It is also commonly called *lamb's lettuce* or *corn salad*. It is not a lettuce, though sheep like to graze upon it. And its only relation to corn (in the British sense of "grain") was proximity in ancient times in the field where both flourished. The leaves are bright spanking green, shaped like tongues or a dog's floppy ears. Mâche may be packaged as separate clean leaves, or with its soft rosettes bunched with soil-covered roots and all. The diminutive leaves are 4 to 6 inches long and about 1½ inches wide.

For all its exalted reputation among savvy cooks, mâche has what you might call a laid-back taste. It has a pleasant grassy-green flavor, akin to that of soft lettuce greens. But it is delicate and does add that intangible *je ne sais quoi* to a salad, making it worthy of its mystique.

Where there is mystique there is cost. Though expensive to buy, it is very easy to grow from seed in your backyard garden and the small plant gives a bountiful yield. It is a hardy green, surviving frost and having a predilection for cool, damp weather. In the market it is available between fall and spring. Though it can and does grow here, most of our market mâche is grown overseas, which seems to underscore the snob appeal of dainty mâche. In

Europe, from Ireland to the Mediterranean, the ancient salad leaf is highly favored.

The soft, young leaves are best. Store in the refrigerator and use them as soon as possible, as their ephemeral qualities are leaching out every moment you delay. If the stems are still intact, cut and discard them and wash the leaves gently.

The soft and succulent leaves can stand on their own or in complementary salad green blends. The mild flavor serves as a foil for more strongly flavored greens, but keep it away from anything so coarse and crisp as iceberg lettuce. Mushrooms, beets, avocado slices, walnuts, crumbled cheeses, and radishes stand the waifish leaves in good stead. If the likes of mâche did not exist, it would have to be invented as a receptacle for nut oils, mustard or lemon dressings, crumbled hard-cooked egg, creamy vinaigrettes, and fruit-flavored and balsamic vinegars, the constructs of today's most sumptuous salads.

Some cookbooks say mâche may also be cooked as spinach is, but what a crime! Its downy texture is so ineffably a part of the mâche experience, it is best not to expunge it through cooking.

Mâche with Pignoli

 *4 servings*

¼ cup extra virgin olive oil
2 tablespoons white wine vinegar
¼ teaspoon Dijon mustard
Pinch white pepper
Salt to taste
4 cups cleaned mâche leaves
2 tablespoons pine nuts (pignoli)

1. In a small bowl, combine oil, vinegar, mustard, pepper, and salt and stir gently.

2. Mound mâche leaves on 4 salad plates. Distribute dressing and nuts over each serving.

ℳalanga

Also called *yautia*, this barrel- or club-shaped root crop resembles the taro (page 131), with which it may often be confused. It has a rough, brown, scaly skin like taro, covering a beige or yam-colored underflesh. Its more emphatic flavor is sweet and nutty and earthy, and its texture is creamy and smooth.

Malanga can be baked, boiled, fried, pureed like potatoes, or made into a sweetened dessertlike treat. It is a good side dish to highly spiced meat, fish, or poultry. Well-seasoned tomato dishes are a good way to serve this starchy tuber.

Like potatoes, malanga is available all year round, usually in stores or produce markets catering to a Latino clientele. It should be fresh-smelling and hard, with no soft or decaying spots. Store it for up to a week in the refrigerator or for no longer than a few days at room temperature. Remove the skin with a paring knife before or after cooking.

Malanga Hash Browns

 *4 servings*

Serve these as an accompaniment to omelets or other egg dishes.

2 pounds malanga, peeled
½ onion, grated

¼ cup vegetable oil
Hot sauce (optional)
Salt and pepper to taste

1. Shred malanga by hand or in a food processor with a shredding disk. Toss with onion.
2. Heat oil in a skillet. Stir in malanga and onion and cook, stirring occasionally, until malanga begins to turn golden. Season with hot sauce, if desired, and salt and pepper.

Mustard Greens

With their spikes of four-petaled yellow blossoms brightly splashing meadows and abandoned city lots, mustard greens are an alluring sight. There are many varieties of mustards, and this one, properly called *India mustard* (*Brassica juncea*) is related to the seeds of the ubiquitous condiment that is the better half of hot dogs. The Oriental mustard green, bok choy (page 78), is also a kin of this hardy member of the Crucifer family.

This plant's jade-green leaves are slightly curled or ruffled, looking crisp as a little girl's freshly starched pinafore. Mustard greens are another vitamin-laden potherb. A 1-cup serving of the cooked greens contains over 8,000 international units of vitamin A, less than 50 calories, almost 200 milligrams of calcium, 68 milligrams of vitamin C, and noteworthy amounts of iron, phosphorus, and B vitamins. Its use in herbal therapy as a mustard plaster for muscle soreness and bronchial congestion is legendary.

Again it is the South that pays more of the deserving homage to this overlooked green. It may be cooked in a jumble with collards, kale, and other such greens or infused with salt pork, bacon, or ham hocks, a concoction that may then be served with black-eyed peas and a healthy wedge of down-home corn bread. Mustard greens are as good in a thin broth with ham chunks as they are pureed in a cream soup with the most assertive of curry spices—cumin, cardamom, coriander, turmeric, mustard, mace, ginger, or chili. Substitute mustard greens for the collards in Dill-Onion-Collard Cheesecake, page 82. The cooking tones the hotness of its raw flavor to a milder cabbage pungency, though of greener note and ever so slight bitterness. Steamed mustard greens go well with potatoes and tomatoes for flavor and nutritional enhancement. Treat mustards as you would any other green, especially Swiss chard, kale, collards, or spinach. A 15- to 20-minute steaming renders the greens tender. From there you can slather them with butter, olive oil, vinegar, garlic. Dill or caraway marry well with their sharpness, too. Use only the small tender sweet ones in salads in tandem with other mild greens.

Although mustard greens are not greatly esteemed in the North, I have always been able to find them there (along with an array of Italian and other less pursued greens) in big farmers' markets year round. Look for bright, jade-green leaves, with a sort of brocade finish. Avoid limp and yellow foliage. Store mustard greens as you would other greens (see page 54) for a few days, as they wilt quickly. Cut away any tough stem ends.

Mustard Greens with Black-Eyed Peas in White Wine

 *4 to 6 servings*

This is a variation on a favorite recipe that I developed for *Attenzione* magazine, March 1984.

½ pound dried black-eyed peas (about 1½ cups)
2 cups dry white wine
3 cups water

1 carrot
1 stalk celery
1 small whole onion, unpeeled
2 bay leaves
1 pound mustard greens, cleaned and coarsely chopped
4 tablespoons sweet butter
3 shallots, minced
3 cloves garlic, minced
1 medium-size sweet pepper, chopped
4 tablespoons flour
1/4 teaspoon ground cloves
1/4 teaspoon crushed red pepper
3/4 teaspoon salt
2 tablespoons drained capers

1. Soak black-eyed peas in a 4-quart pot with enough water to cover by 2 inches for at least 6 hours or overnight. Drain and add wine, 3 cups of water, carrot, celery, onion, and bay leaves to the peas. Bring to a boil, then lower heat and simmer for 50 minutes. Add greens and simmer another 20 minutes, until greens are very tender. Drain, reserving 1 1/2 cups of the cooking liquid. Remove carrot, celery, onion, and bay leaves and discard.

2. Heat butter in a saucepan, then add shallots, garlic, and sweet pepper, and cook until soft, about 5 minutes. Stir in flour until a smooth paste forms, then slowly stir in bean liquid. Add cloves, crushed pepper, and salt. Cook sauce over low heat until thickened, about 7 minutes. Stir in capers.

3. Combine sauce with beans and greens and turn into a serving dish. Serve as an accompaniment to roasted meat, fish, or poultry.

Nopales

In Mexico and parts of Central America the pads of the prickly pear cactus plant, or nopales, are considered a culinary treat. This may sound unrefined, but the marinated, depricked plant is quite a delicacy in those areas. The best description of this interesting treat is a flavor akin to that of artichoke hearts, string beans, or lima beans, with a mucilaginous texture similar to that of okra. As with okra, there are few lukewarm reactions to nopales: people "love 'em or leave 'em."

Yet nopales are a tasty and very interesting addition to the increasingly popular southwestern cuisine. They can be added to soups, warmed as a side dish vegetable, or added to omelets, casseroles, salads, or any vegetable medley. Since they are so mild, they go well steeped in a spicy Salsa Cruda (see recipe, page 140).

Nopales are sold fresh, canned, or *en escabeche,* as they are called when pickled. They are available where Mexican foods are sold. The fresh ones are in peak form in spring. It is the tender young cactus pad that is most desirable, not the larger pads (all are depricked before going to market). They should be bright green with a firm, crisp skin, not dry, wilted, or shriveled.

To use the fresh ones, poke out the "eyes" and any remaining stickers and tough or fibrous patches before preparing. Enjoy fresh nopales raw or boiled in salted water, sautéed, or steamed like a fresh vegetable. Do not overcook. They are good with assertive seasonings—tomatoes, onions, chilies, oregano, sharp cheeses— but also appreciated when unadorned for their mild, fresh herb flavor.

Picante Nopales-Nachos Dip

 *6 to 8 servings*

Here is a way to introduce newcomers to this unusual treat.

1 recipe Salsa de Chili Rojo (see page 72)
1½ cups shredded cheddar or Monterey Jack cheese
1 cup canned nopales, diced
Corn chips

Heat the salsa almost to a boil. Stir in cheese until melted and incorporated into salsa. Stir in nopales and pour into crock or serving bowl. Serve as a dip with corn chips.

Okra

Okra pods look like the prehistoric vegetable they are, having originated on the fertile plains of what is today Ethiopia. Silt wasn't the only natural treasure found along the Nile. Wild okra (*Hibiscus esculentus*) still grows there today. Okra made its way to Arabia and Egypt with Moslem conquerors and with slaves to the Caribbean. The French brought it to the Mississippi delta. Soup manufacturers got it into cans, where its controversial gummy quality makes all jell. Commercially, okra is grown in Florida, Texas, Georgia, and New Jersey. The plant's pretty yellow and red-centered flowers are also a common sight in gardens in Louisiana, a state where cooks understand the good in the gooeyness of okra.

Okra pods look like little rockets, but instead of fuselage, they have mucilage, the damning or endearing characteristic, depending on your preference. The descriptive name *ladyfinger* also traveled with okra, as did *gumbo*, an African name, which now implies the most famous dish it appears in. These pocket-size rockets or digitals are lime-green and often have a velvety feel. Inside the ridged pods are rows of tiny seeds in their slippery membrane sack. This rather innocuous gelatinous texture may turn many Americans outside the South off, but the Greeks, Turks, Indians, and other Middle Easterners are not such okraphobes. They use it any way you can imagine—boiled, baked, fried with meat, onions, tomatoes, or other vegetables. Americans enjoy fat slick in their food (as statistics indicate), so I don't know what they have against this cellulose slip—actually a type of fiber with health benefits.

Okra may be sliced into little hub caps or left whole. Indians curry or stuff whole okra with exotic spices. West Indian *callaloo*, a soup made with hearty greens and also of African origin, relies on okra's thickening power.

In America, the South has its stamp on okra dishes. In addition to a panoply of thick and rich gumbo recipes, there are crispy, succulent okra fritters made with a cornmeal batter, a delicious snack. Okra and black-eyed peas are a nutritious and delicious combination, and the whole okra pods may be pickled with hot peppers. The vegetable hubs can be sautéed with a little butter and garlic or stewed with a tomato, pepper, and onion medley. Okra also goes well with summer squashes. It needs only a good ten minutes in any soup or stew to infuse its thickening magic.

Look for small okra, not bigger than 2½ to 3 inches. They range up to 7 inches long, at which point they begin to resemble their tough and fibrous kin, cotton and hemp (all in the same mallow family). Avoid too much rust color on their close-cropped furry skin, and of course shriveling should deter your interest. The pods should have a crisp green-bean snap to them. They are available year round, with mid- to late summer their peak appearance.

They are very perishable, so try to use them within a day of purchase. Wash them just before preparing and cut the woody stem ends off, but only at the last moment, or the pods will quickly ooze their gluey humors.

Okra Tempura

 *4 to 6 servings*

1¼ cups flour
½ teaspoon baking powder
1 egg, beaten
1 cup milk
½ teaspoon salt
½ teaspoon black pepper
Oil for deep-frying (about 1 quart)
1 pound okra pods, cleaned and trimmed

1. Combine flour and baking powder in a small bowl. Add egg, milk, salt, and pepper and stir until well mixed. Let stand 1 hour.
2. Prepare oil for deep-frying. Fill deep fryer or deep 2-quart pot with at least 3 inches of oil. Heat oil to 375°F., testing with deep-frying thermometer if necessary. Do not allow oil to smoke. Dip okra into batter, then lower into hot oil. The coated vegetable should sizzle immediately. Cook until nicely browned, about 1 minute for each pod. Cook several pods at a time, but do not crowd them or they will cook unevenly. Remove browned pods with a slotted spoon and drain on lots of paper toweling. Serve immediately with any dipping or barbecue sauce.

Radicchio

Radicchio's brilliantly striated mauve and ivory leaves are beautiful to behold. A food photographer's love is to capture the leaf's red-and-cream marble smoothness in chic still-life pose. Is it mere coincidence that this rococo *Cichorium intybus* hails from the Venetian province, a noted hotbed of the world's most astonishingly sensual art?

Radicchio resembles a miniature purple cabbage that has been bleached along its ribs. The leaves are as stiff as a crisp raw cabbage leaf, too. A head ranges from the size of a golf ball to that of a grapefruit. Radicchio, also called *red chicory*, is actually a flaming cousin to Belgian endive, with which it shares an equal quotient of bitterness. Radicchio may have slightly more assertiveness, but it's undebatably got the visual flair that counts for so much with today's cook's sensibility. And it's got the price. At 4 to 6 dollars per pound it is not uncommon for people to blanch at the sight of red chicory.

There are several varieties of radicchio, but it is the rounder *radicchio di Verona* that is exported to the United States from Italy. *Radicchio di Treviso*, with long tapered leaves, is also popular. You may see the variegated chicory of *Castelfranco*, a larger globe with green speckles in addition to the fiery streaks.

In northern Europe radicchio is a staple during the winter. In Treviso and Venice, the radicchio region, a salad based solely on the two-toned leaf is not uncommon. Radicchio has the stamina to be oiled and cooked on a grill, an unusual and satisfying use for the red chicory. Although its firmness will go flaccid, the way grilled peppers do, and it will lose its flamboyant color; radicchio's subtler cooked taste is very appealing and better suited to use in pasta dishes, omelets, rice dishes, or as a warm salad. The durable uncooked leaves can be turned into edible ramekins to fill with salads. Radicchio's showiness and bittersweet flavor stand out in a mixed salad and complement other greens, especially any of the New Age salad ones—mâche, redleaf lettuce, arugula, and watercress. Creamy sharp vinaigrettes, balsamic vinegar, and flavored oils are a good match for the peppery leaf.

Red chicory is available year round from Italy, Mexico, and our East and West Coast growers, though, as you might expect, the more costly imported stuff is more in demand. Check the stem base of the head for firmness and damage. Make sure there is no drying or browning at the leaf's edge. At the price you're paying, it should look as sleek as Carrara marble. It stores well for a good solid week, maybe longer, in the refrigerator.

Rice Salad with Eggplant and Radicchio
Risotto, Radicchio, e Melanzana

 *6 servings*

1 small eggplant
½ cup olive oil
1 small head radicchio (about 10 leaves), sliced into ½-inch
  strips
2½ cups cooked long-grain rice
1 small sweet red pepper, cut into thin strips
½ pound mozzarella, cut into ½-inch cubes
Juice of 1 whole lemon
1 clove garlic, crushed
2 tablespoons chopped fresh basil
2 tablespoons chopped fresh parsley
½ teaspoon salt
¼ teaspoon fresh ground pepper
½ cup virgin olive oil

1. Preheat oven to 400°F. Wash eggplant and slice into ¾-inch rounds, then quarter each round. Toss eggplant wedges with

¼ cup olive oil until all pieces are well coated. Spread wedges in single layer on a baking sheet and roast for 10 minutes, or until golden brown; turn pieces over and brown other side. Set aside to cool.

2. Brush radicchio strips liberally with remaining ¼ cup olive oil. Spread on baking sheet and roast for 5 to 7 minutes, turning once. Radicchio should be soft and limp.

3. Toss together rice, sliced pepper, and cheese.

4. In a small bowl, combine remaining ingredients. Pour over rice mixture and toss again. Add cooled eggplant and radicchio (reserve a few pieces to garnish top of salad), gently toss to avoid mashing eggplant. Serve chilled or at room temperature.

Rutabaga

The rutabaga is not a turnip, though its parentage on one side traces back to the turnip during medieval times. It is a member of the Brassica family, its taste noticeably determined by its heritage. Some confusion between the two vegetables may come from the fact that the rutabaga is also called a *Swedish turnip*, *Swede*, or *yellow turnip*. The root vegetable does resemble an oversized turnip, but the rutabaga has a much plumper neck and purplish mahogany skin, while turnips are white with purple tint. A rutabaga has yellow flesh that is denser than the turnip's more watery ivory flesh.

In *Buying Produce* (Hearst Books, 1986), Jack Murdich calls the rutabaga a "humble vegetable with a heart of gold," not an unusual temperament for the misbegotten. For unclear reasons, the rutabaga, with its earthy cabbage flavor, has never inspired mass appeal. Perhaps it is because children don't have great affinity for it, and adults just don't want to bother with the oafish bulb. This is unfortunate, since it has a bargain price and is a good source of fiber, vitamin A, and calcium.

The rutabaga is starchier than the turnip and its most common usage is as a creamy textured puree, popular in Europe, much like mashed potatoes here. The velvety puree (the rutabaga is not stringy like many squashes) can be enriched with cheese, cream, butter, and spices. Such modifiers make the puree nice company for fowl and game. The rutabaga can also be used just like the turnip—sautéed, steamed and buttered, or added to a heartwarming soup broth to impart its pleasant, full-bodied flavor. With other vegetables, diced cooked rutabaga can be made into a salad similar to potato salad. The vegetable is also compatible with sweet seasonings; some brown sugar or honey and yogurt make a nice foil for its pudding attributes.

Canada and California grow rutabagas, the former supplying the better crop. They are in season from fall through summer. Select round, heavy rutabagas that are about as hard as a butcher block.

It is a common practice to encase the root in paraffin to extend its shelf life. Produce dealers seem to know the rutabaga will be hanging around for quite a few months. The wax comes off with the skin, which peels off as easily as a turnip's. Gardeners store the hardy vegetable for up to six months under cool, moist conditions. You can keep your rutabaga in the refrigerator for up to two weeks.

Golden Puree of Rutabaga

 *4 servings*

1 large rutabaga (about 1½ pounds)
½ cup heavy cream
¼ cup grated Gruyère cheese
1 tablespoon grated Parmesan
2 tablespoons chopped fresh parsley

2 tablespoons chopped fresh chives
¼ teaspoon white pepper

1. Pare rutabaga and slice into 1-inch pieces. Steam until tender, about 35 minutes.

2. When cooled slightly, place rutabaga in food processor fitted with metal blade. Process until a very smooth puree. Slowly add cream and process again. Add cheeses and pulse 3 or 4 times just to mix. Turn puree into chafing dish and stir in parsley, chives, and pepper. Reheat in a moderate oven, if necessary, and serve hot.

Salsify (Oyster Plant)

On a recent trip to southern France I pleaded with my French friends to find me some *salsifis*. They were puzzled by my zeal for the low-keyed root they've known since childhood. They have little interest in the vegetable, which is easy enough to get there, while it is elevated to specialty status in this country. Times used to be better and worse for salsify. The plant was once a home cook's staple here, then became all but extinct, a pre- and post–World War II phenomenon. There's no doubt that wars change things, in this case the populace's taste for salsify. But now food-scene watchers predict the hairy root vegetable is coming back here and losing ground in Europe. If this is correct, my French friends will soon be asking me to hunt down some *salsifis* for them.

Salsify, often called *oyster plant* or *oyster vegetable*, has been around for centuries. The ancient Greeks and Romans gathered it, and it was thriving in Europe for ages, then too in North America when colonists got wind of its antibilious and diuretic herbal qualities. The French and Germans used it a lot in their cuisine, while the English appreciated the plant as an ornamental.

Salsify (*Tragopogon porrifolius*) is rarely mentioned without scorzonera (*Scorzonera hispanica*), which may be called *black salsify*. Both belong to the same Compositae family and are considered interchangeable by most cooks. Both are long tapering roots, like carrots, though the black one is more slender, cylindrical, and less snarled and hairy. Salsify has parsnip-yellow skin; scorzonera's is brown to black. They're both 6 to 8 inches long and about 1 inch in diameter, with crisp ivory flesh.

Cooks of one age believed that salsify tasted like oysters, which is why the bivalve lent its name to the vegetable. Most modern cooks seem to disagree with this taste description, though I'm not sure I do. It may require a stretch of the imagination, but I will add to the indecision that I think the cooked root tastes something like sea scallops, sultry sweet and buttery textured. However you describe salsify, it most definitely has that elusive delicacy, unique to certain other vegetables, such as asparagus, globe artichoke hearts, and perhaps Jerusalem artichokes.

It is unfortunate that since World War II salsify is not seen very often in markets. It's imported from Belgium and Holland, of course with a "designer" vegetable price tag. Perhaps the renewed interest here will change this.

Salsify may be enjoyed raw, but it is more common to boil or steam it. It cooks in 20 to 30 minutes if you boil or in about an hour if you steam, depending on the thickness of slices. I first enjoyed salsify in France, cooked and marinated in a brine, as part of a cold salad tray along with carrots and beets *râpés*, cold boiled potatoes, corn, a macédoine salad, and hard-cooked eggs, served with a mustard vinaigrette. It was delectable.

A dressing with anchovy paste brings out salsify's shellfish taste. The tender cooked fleshy vegetable mates well with any type of cheese sauce or butter sauce. Parboil it first, then bake it with the sauce. It is delicious in an au gratin composition. The white salsify breaks easily, so handle it carefully. It's a good idea to peel this one after it's been boiled or steamed and is cool enough to handle. Serve it cold with oil and lemon for a quick side dish or warm with a nut oil dressing. A mornay sauce is a richer and dressier guise. Some cookbooks suggest treating salsify as you would rutabagas, turnips, and parsnips. I think you may want to wait until their price is in the same pedestrian league before you treat this root too commonly.

The delicate flavor naturally suggests pureeing the root into a velvety cream soup. It can also be mixed with bread crumbs and flavorings and made into fritters. A mock oyster stew sounds like an irreproachable sleight of hand.

Salsify is at your disposal from autumn to early spring. Choose firm smooth roots that suggest a crisp juicy flesh interior. Avoid wrinkled, limp, or flabby ones. Sometimes the vegetable appears with its grasslike leaf tops, which can be cooked like other greens or added to soup for their mild flavor. Store salsify as you would carrots, in plastic in the vegetable crisper.

To prepare salsify, trim the ends, then scrub and scrape the roots before cooking or after blanching. Since it oxidizes rapidly, slice the vegetable into water acidulated with 1 tablespoon of lemon juice or vinegar for each cup of liquid.

Like Jerusalem artichokes, oyster plants store their carbohydrates as inulin, making them another good starch for diabetics.

Salsify, Peas, and Chicken

 *4 servings*

2 thin strips bacon, chopped
1 small onion, minced
1 pound black or white salsify, peeled and thinly sliced
1 10-ounce package frozen peas
1½ pounds boned, skinless chicken breast, cut into bite-size
   pieces
½ teaspoon thyme
Salt and pepper to taste

1. Sauté bacon and onion in a large skillet until bacon is almost crisp. Add salsify and sauté another 10 minutes.

2. Stir in peas, chicken, and thyme and sauté until chicken is cooked through, about 7 minutes. Season to taste. Serve immediately with rice or buttered noodles.

Sorrel

The Romans, like the Greeks, never overlooked a medicinal herb. They surely found one in sorrel, with its impressive roster of minerals and high vitamin C content. Innovative cooks of today have given this same sour grass that the Romans used for many common ailments a permanent niche in the new American cuisine.

The plant contains a good deal of a compound called oxalate of potash, which lends the characteristic sharp, sour taste, an acquired taste for some. Sorrel's name derives from a French word meaning sour, hence its other name, *sour grass*.

The French sorrel (*Rumex scutatus*) we can find in markets, with its deep-clover-green leaves, is most often grown in hothouses. The entire plant or just the arrowhead-shaped leaves may be sold, since the plants are prolific producers and regenerators of leaves. Unfortunately, the leaves wilt swiftly after being cut. But even the tired foliage of this potherb retains the distinct sharpness. Young tender leaves are better than the older tough ones. If you grow the plant, harvest the leaves anytime—the more often the better—and the plant will send you back a new treasure trove of tender tasty leaves.

Sorrel has a time-honored tradition in the kitchen. The old English pease porridge needs sorrel to be authentic. But sorrel is also one of those forgotten ingredients coming back into its own, and with good reason. Sorrel renders a powerful sharp puree, that with the sweet of cream melds into a creation greater than the sum of its parts. This unique sour taste in a pureed sauce or as a dressing herb is becoming a striking classic with fish, particularly salmon and trout. Cream of sorrel soup already has high favor as a new American classic, often as a lavish prelude to a luxurious meal.

Sorrel has steadfast versatility as both vegetable and herb. Sorrel leaves added to potatoes in butter transform that ordinary pleasure into something special. With the counterpoint of creamy avocado, mild soft cheese, or bosky mushrooms, sorrel gives omelets a new twist. Sorrel puree can stand in spinach's stead for Florentine dishes. Raw sorrel adds a pleasant acid note when mixed with mild lettuce in salads. Just like spinach, sorrel can behave as a stuffing for rabbit or chicken, a common role in France.

Sorrel is available in fall, winter, and spring. The leaves should be lush, full, and vividly green, with no signs of wilt or yellow. Wash them well, and spin or blot them dry with paper towel. Trim the stems. Store in the refrigerator's vegetable crisper for a couple days or, more ideally, use them immediately.

Broiled Salmon with Sorrel Sauce

 *4 servings*

½ cup dry white wine
¼ cup sherry wine vinegar
2 tablespoons minced shallots
5 tablespoons butter
1½ cups packed shredded sorrel leaves
1 cup light cream
4 6-ounce salmon steaks
1 tablespoon lemon juice
¼ teaspoon salt
Freshly ground black pepper

1. Combine wine, vinegar, and shallots in small saucepan. Cook over moderately high heat, until liquid is reduced to 2 tablespoons.

2. Heat 2 tablespoons butter in another saucepan. Stir in sorrel and cook until wilted, about 2 minutes. Puree in blender or food processor with 1/4 cup of the cream. Add sorrel puree to reduced wine mixture along with remaining cream. Cook until slightly thickened, then remove from heat.

3. Place salmon steaks under broiler and broil for 5 to 8 minutes, until fish flakes easily with a fork and flesh is opaque throughout.

4. Meanwhile, reheat sorrel sauce, whisking in remaining butter, lemon juice, salt, and pepper to taste. Transfer salmon to serving plate and spoon sauce over fish. Serve immediately.

Swiss Chard (Chard)

My grandmother always included Swiss chard in her garden of lively Italian vegetables. A summer or fall visit from any of her grandchildren prompted a scurry to the refrigerator, where she'd produce, along with the leftover meatballs or veal cutlets and home-cured olives, an enamel pot of *cucuzza*, or Italian ratatouille, and a bowl full of the steamed and sautéed chard greens.

Having inherited her garden, I have continued her practice of growing chard, because the curly emerald leaves with snow-white ribs flourish very easily from seed. I pick the billowy, quiltlike leaves when they are young and tender and cook them briefly in a bamboo steamer (unlike my grandmother, who boiled them and lost more nutrients). No matter how much I strip the plant of its leaves it keeps repaying me generously with new ones.

The name of this vegetable is a mystery to most, no Swiss connection having been unearthed. Swiss chard is actually a type of beet used for its leaves rather than for its root—notice the similarity to beet greens next time you see the two at the produce stand. Both the beet and Swiss chard share a common ancestor in a wild European plant, though the chard developed without the fleshy bulbous root that we call beet. There are green and red types of chard. The green has white midribs, the red has rhubarb-red midribs. I cannot detect any taste differences according to color, only according to size. The smaller leaves are the most succulent and toothsome. Both the stalks and the leaves are good for eating.

A kitchen steamy with the aroma of cooking Swiss chard always evokes my Proustian memories of comfort food, thanks to my grandmother, no doubt. Or maybe the delicate flavor fresh from the garden does this for everyone. It is a subtle but full-bodied green, like a very fresh spinach, but dewier and not as sharp, though sometimes slightly bitter. Its very health-giving profile reinforces this impression, with a high vitamin A and C content and notable amounts of calcium and iron.

I feel the steamed chard needs no further ado when very fresh. The young leaves can be added to salad, too, with no cooking. When I buy the larger mature leaves from a market, for a bit more pungency I bathe them in the garlic and olive oil standby after steaming. I have learned some other ways to bring out Swiss chard's best, from cooks other than my grandmother. At Chez Panisse in Berkeley, Alice Waters serves a crusty calzone filled with a medley of cheeses, bits of ham, and Swiss chard. I liked this combination so much I re-created my own version at home. Another Swiss chard inspiration came from a friend who stuffed the large leaves with a vegetable filling and covered all with a savory tomato sauce.

Chard's subdued tartness mingles easily with most anything from cream to tomatoes. A Mediterranean-style recipe with nuts and dried fruit plays off these tart attributes, sometimes with a sweetener added. Chard leaves may be included in soups or stir-fried dishes. Like cardoons, the vegetable can be enriched with a nutmeg-flavored béchamel or velouté. It can also be grilled, like radicchio.

Look for very crisply curled bright-green leaves that are not too large. You'll never find anything smaller than 10 to 12 inches in the market; for smaller ones, grow your own. Chard is in from summer through fall. It seems to be making more than a casual appearance in many markets, though this depends on where you live. Wrap it in plastic and refrigerate for up to three days.

Lentil-and-Rice-Stuffed Swiss Chard
with Tomato Sauce

 *4 to 6 servings*

The idea for this delicious spicy recipe came from my friend Betty Stechmeyer, who lives in Mendocino, California, and grows "elephant-sized" leaves of chard there.

2 cups cooked lentils
1 cup cooked brown rice
¼ cup vegetable oil
½ cup chopped walnuts
¼ cup raisins
2 tablespoons whole wheat flour
2 carrots, grated
¼ cup minced green pepper
¼ cup minced onions
½ cup chopped fresh parsley
½ teaspoon crushed red pepper
½ teaspoon cinnamon
¼ teaspoon cardamom
¼ teaspoon turmeric
½ teaspoon salt
15 large Swiss chard leaves
3 cups spicy tomato sauce

1. Combine all ingredients except Swiss chard and sauce. Mix well.
2. Steam Swiss chard leaves for 3 to 5 minutes to soften them. Cut away any tough parts of leaves. Place about ¼ cup of filling at the base of each leaf, roll up and place seam-side down in an oiled baking dish and cover with sauce.
3. Bake at 350°F. for 30 minutes. Serve hot.

Taro

Taro (*Colicasia antiquorum*) is one of the many (and often confusing) species of tubers grown in the humid tropics and known as the yam family. It has large leaves that are also used in the cuisine of certain countries, such as India, where they are stuffed. The starchy Hawaiian paste called *poi* is made from taro roots. Poi is very bland and not often a dining favorite of newcomers to its elusive flavor.

Taro has barklike skin and, like malanga and cassava, its crisp flesh has notes on the sweet and nutty scale, but with subtle differences.

Like other tubers, taro can be simply boiled, baked, or fried, all of which turn its off-white flesh to a pale grayish-violet color. Added to highly seasoned soups, stews, casseroles, it soaks up flavors. Its cooked texture is dry, making it quite receptive to a little sauce or butter. It can also be pureed like potatoes, yams, or squash and made into any dishes in which those vegetables work well.

Caveat: Taro must be eaten cooked, never raw, as it contains a poisonous substance that must be deactivated with heat. The uncooked substance may also irritate sensitive skin.

Asian and Latin markets are apt to carry taro just about all year round. Select the larger, more flavorful specimens. They should be heavy, firm, and free of softness or decay. Store at room temperature, in a potato bin if possible, for up to three to four days. Be sure to use before any rotting occurs.

Basic Boiled Taro

 *4 servings*

3 to 4 medium-size corms of taro

Place unpeeled corms of taro in pot, cover with water, and bring to a boil. Cook for about 25 minutes, until taro is tender to touch of a fork. Drain, slice open, and serve taro with any of the following: butter, salt and pepper, sour cream or yogurt, Salsa Cruda (page 140), Salsa de Chili Rojo (page 72), or any sauce or topping desired.

Tomatillo

Tomatillos, native to Mexico, are not tomatoes, although they are often called *Mexican tomatoes, husk tomatoes,* or *green tomatoes.* They belong to the same nightshade family as tomatoes, but they are actually related to the ground cherry, also called the *Cape gooseberry,* a fruit used for jams and jellies. The tomatillo looks like a small green tomato, but behaves differently in cooking. The tomatillo is seedy but firm, with no juicy cavities such as those found in tomatoes, and the flesh may be purplish at times. It grows to about twice the size of a cherry tomato. When ripe, it is light green and encased in a parchment husk that is easily peeled away. The dry papery husk resembles a Chinese Lantern, another name for a closely related large berry.

Tomatillos, a staple in Mexican cooking, are a star ingredient in several salsas, the very heart and soul of many Mexican dishes. Salsa verde (see following recipe), the mild to hot green sauce served over chili rellenos and tacos, and salsa cruda, an uncooked sauce for many Mexican concoctions, both rely on tomatillos for body and zest.

Unfortunately, outside of Mexican communities, tomatillos are hard to find. However, the growing attention cooks are giving to American regional fare, such as southwestern, has sparked widespread interest. So tomatillos and other Mexican food items may be available in the mainstream markets more and more. Right now, markets in Latin communities are most apt to sell them.

Tomatillos may be used raw, but they are better cooked to bring out their tart berry assets and to soften their sturdy flesh. When eaten raw, they are sharp and acid and may go well in a cold chicken, meat, or vegetable salad. They function best in a sauce with any line of aromatics—garlic, red tomatoes, onions, leeks, chilies, oregano, cilantro. The zesty sauce is just right for many Mexican favorites. You can also add chopped tomatillos to Mexican pinto bean soup, a popular and substantial dish. Mole verde, a rich green sauce for chicken, is worth the search for tomatillos. You can bake whole tomatillos and store them for later use in a recipe. Some cooks recommend interchanging tomatillos and green tomatoes, but this should only be done as a last resort.

Look for the brittle-husked lanterns year round in Hispanic communities or in specialty shops. The flesh should look firm and smooth, like an unripe green tomato still clinging to its vine. It should wear its husk slightly loose, with no brown spots of decay. Store tomatillos in the refrigerator for up to three weeks or longer if they are still in good shape. You can also stew them and freeze for later use in sauces, or can them as you would tomatoes.

Salsa Verde

 *Makes about 1¾ cups*

8 tomatillos
¼ cup chopped white onions
1 California chili, roasted, peeled, and seeded
1 tablespoon chopped cilantro
1 tablespoon olive oil
1 tablespoon white wine vinegar
1 teaspoon minced garlic
¼ teaspoon sugar
¼ teaspoon salt
¼ teaspoon black pepper

1. Remove husks from tomatillos and wash. Place tomatillos in saucepan, cover with water, and bring to boil. Lower heat and simmer 7 minutes.

2. Drain tomatillos, combine with onions, chili, and cilantro and puree in blender or food processor. Combine with remaining ingredients. Store in refrigerator and serve at room temperature.

CHILI PEPPERS

With the rise of interest in exotic cuisines, fiery chilies are gaining acceptance from America's once puerile taste buds. As our palates become more sophisticated, we realize that a chili's contribution transcends the addition of mere hotness. Consider its well-integrated role with the perfume of lemongrass and coconut cream in Thai cuisine, with an earthy exotic Indian curry of eighteen spices, or laced through a Chinese dish with ginger, garlic, and sesame. How different each role is. Vietnamese, Korean, and other Asian cuisines are equally cognizant of the chili's characteristics. Mexican and Latin American cuisines have long been almost synonymous with chili peppers. All this receptiveness to the potentially volatile chili has paved the way for our own Southwest and Tex-Mex cooking to gain more popularity. The quest, now that we appreciate the versatile chili, is to distinguish and understand the differences in the piquancy and seasoning of the many (often easily confused) chilies.

ABOUT CHILIES

Botanically, chilies are fruits, not seeds like peppercorns. Their incendiary attributes are due to the presence of an alkaloid called capsaicin. Ironically this ingredient, which makes some people's hair stand on end, is the subject of research for painkillers at the University of California at San Francisco. Dr. Jon Levine has shown that in laboratory animals capsaicin lessens the pain of inflammation. Apparently the substance eventually numbs pain fibers until they don't respond to the painful stimulus—much the way people build a tolerance for branding-iron hot chili peppers. More research is needed, though, before the seasoning is moved from the kitchen to the medicine chest.

Peppers are well known for their high amounts of vitamin A and of several important minerals, but most especially for their vitamin C content.

Mexican and Oriental markets are the most reliable sources for fresh chilies, although more and more large supermarkets are beginning to carry a good selection. Fresh chilies are available from midsummer through fall, and the dried ones can usually be found in specialty stores year round. Store the fresh ones in a paper bag in the refrigerator for up to one week and the dried ones in a dark place indefinitely.

TIPS FOR HANDLING CHILIES

As a rule, green chilies (the unripened fruit of any variety) are more devilish than red, ripened chilies. Red chilies have sweetened slightly with maturity. In general, narrow pointed pods indicate hotness, and the smaller the chili, the more scorching it's likely to be. Broader, more rounded pods (such as the bell pepper's) lean toward sweetness. Small, narrow jalapeños and serranos, the most popular hot chilies in Tex-Mex cooking, are quite piping to most American palates.

Restraint is advisable. Always add chili or chili-seasoned sauces to any dish in small amounts at first. The unpredictable spiciness may not be apparent until it is released fully in the cooking process, so taste the food continually as you prepare it.

Combine chili with other ingredients in any dish to diffuse some of its hotness. Salt, sweeteners, and acid ingredients such as tomatoes, vinegar, and lemon juice all help to soften the sting and to bring out its distinctive bouquet. The chili's bite is confined largely to its seeds and veins (or ribs), which you can easily remove to achieve a milder flavor; soaking chilies in salted ice water or milk for about an hour is also effective.

PREPARING FRESH AND DRIED CHILIES

When handling hot chilies, wear thin gloves to protect your hands from the volatile oils. Do not touch your face or eyes for a while, even after you've washed your hands—the irritant is persistent and may still be present.

If you use fresh chilies, it may be necessary to first roast, peel, and seed them for many dishes. The roasting heightens their flavor and enables you to remove the cellophane-like skin. The stem and seeds can be removed before or after roasting. Place the chilies on a baking sheet under the broiler for 3 to 5 minutes, until the outer skins blister and char in several spots. Remove from the oven, put in a plastic bag, and place them in the freezer for 5 minutes. When the chilies are cool enough to handle, the skins will peel off very easily.

Dried chilies, popular in the West and Southwest, are more difficult to find in other parts of the country. However, you may be able to find ground chilies (not the same as "chili powder," the spice blend). You can also prepare dried chilies in advance and store the paste in a jar in the refrigerator for up to three months. If you prefer a mild sauce, use the dried Anaheim (or New Mexican) chili for this procedure. Remove the chilies' stems, shake out and discard the seeds. Tear the chilies into smaller strips and place on a baking sheet in a preheated 325°F. oven for 7 minutes. Transfer the chilies to a bowl and add enough water to cover them; allow them to sit for an hour, then puree them along with the soak water in small patches. You now have a chili paste that can be used to season salsas, soup, beans, rice, eggs, and other dishes.

Anaheim   Also called *long green, red chili, California long green, chile verde*, or *New Mexico chili*, the Anaheim is light green to dark bright green and ripens to red. Six to 7 inches long and 1 to 2 inches wide, the Anaheim is mild to slightly hot. Dried maroon Anaheims are threaded into the festive ropes of *ristras* you may see all over shops in the Southwest and in Mexico. Anaheim is one of the most popular relleno chilies. It is used fresh, roasted and peeled first, for stuffing and sauces. Its flavor is one of the most neutral of chilies, which makes it the favorite of less macho taste buds. It is often the chili of choice for the popular red or green sauces that accompany every other dish in Mexican cooking. This chili of the masses can be easily added to any dish in strips or chopped in to wake up any simple egg, vegetable, meat, chicken, or fish dish.

Ancho   This glossy mahogany-brown chili is the poblano chili (see page 139), all dried up and wrinkled. It is 3 to 5 inches long and about 2½ to 3 inches wide and mild to slightly hot. To confuse chili seekers further, the ancho may be called *mulato* or *pasilla*. Rehydrated, it becomes crimson again and has a sweet fruitlike flavor that is nice in many sauces, including mole and Mexican salsas.

Cascabel   This small, round, barnyard-red chili with its smooth skin is about 1½ inches in diameter. Named for its loose rattling seeds, which give the impression of a jingle bell or maraca, the cascabel is moderately hot, with a nutty flavor that comes to the fore with toasting. This chili, used in its dried form in the United States, is best in sauces and with meat.

Chipotle   This chili, actually a smoke-dried jalapeño, can be a two-tone brown or a brick red and is 2 to 3 inches long and about

¾ inch wide. It is very hot to searing and has no substitutes in the chili clan. The characteristic flavor of the chipotle comes from the smoke-drying process. Chipotles come from Mexico dried, *en escabeche* (pickled), and in tomato sauce. Chipotles add their fire and smoky spiciness to chili con carne and barbecue sauces. They are a good chili flavoring for mild bean, rice, corn, or cheese dishes.

Hungarian Yellow Wax   This hot banana pepper starts as a pale chartreuse that turns orange, then ripens to scarlet on the vine. A long tapering chili, it is 4 to 6 inches in length and about 1 inch in width and is pungently hot to stinging. The sweet variety is called the *banana pepper* and the hot one, the *yellow wax pepper*. The latter is good in salsas, salads, and pickled vegetables. When it is bright orange, its flavor is at peak. Test the heat of the chili to see if it is sweet or hot. Dice it fresh into salads, soups, sauces, casseroles, or dressings.

Jalapeño   A waxy bright to dark green or purplish chili that ripens to golden and scarlet, the jalapeño is about 2½ to 3 inches long and ½ inch wide. It has a good biting sting that is often straight fire. It is most often used when green and mature and is commonly pickled. It is good in relishes, salsas, soups, salads, with meat, poultry, fish, and in many vegetable medleys. It is the standard zest of the ever-popular appetizer nachos.

Pequin   This pea-size oval is pure hotness and should be used very sparingly. It ripens from green to red and can be dried to a bright shiny brown. It is about ½ inch long and ¼ inch wide and is used commercially as Tabasco and cayenne or in vinegared hot sauces.

Poblano   This chili is dark evergreen, ripening to a rich reddish brown. The handsome, heart-shaped chili is about 4 to 5 inches long and 2 to 3 inches wide and mild to fairly hot. It is a good relleno stuffing pepper when green and mature. Soups, stews, and sauces can also benefit from the pungency of its thick flesh when roasted and peeled. The rich flavor, reminiscent of bell peppers, deepens as this chili ripens, when it may be dried into ancho chilies.

Serrano   The serrano is light to dark green and scarlet red when ripened. Only 1½ to 2 inches long and ½ inch wide, this small pointed chili is nonetheless fairly hot to infernolike. Most often used in the green mature stage when it has the most pungently fruity flavor, it is sometimes believed interchangeable with jalapeños, though the latter are a bit less lively. Serranos may be green and red or orange-streaked. They are available as dried pods, too. They are good in guacamole, relishes, sauces, pickles, and most any dish worthy of bite and spice.

Small Red Pepper (Cayenne Pepper)   Bright green to bright red when ripened, this long chili ranges from 3 to 8 inches in length and up to ¾ inch in width. Hot and fiery, this thin-fleshed chili can substitute for serranos or jalapeños. It is often dried and ground and sold as a powder.

Other chilies of more irregular appearance in the market include the guajillo, guero, hot cherry, mulato, pasilla, sandia, tepin, and Thai, in various degrees of heat and flavor.

Salsa Cruda

 *Makes 1¾ cups*

4 very ripe tomatoes
2 serrano or Anaheim chilies, roasted, peeled, seeded, and finely chopped
2 tablespoons minced onion
1 tablespoon olive oil
¼ teaspoon minced garlic

Juice of 1 lime
1 tablespoon chopped fresh cilantro
¼ teaspoon black pepper, ground
¼ teaspoon salt

Place tomatoes in a bowl and add enough boiling water to cover. Allow to sit 10 minutes, then drain. Remove tomato skins. Slice tomatoes in half horizontally, spoon out seeds, chop finely, and combine with remaining ingredients.

Baked Chilaquiles

 *6 to 8 servings*

This is a popular Mexican dish made with leftover tortillas. Substitute a spicier chili, if you prefer.

6 corn tortillas, cut into 1-inch strips
1¼ cups grated Monterey Jack cheese
3 to 4 Anaheim chilies, roasted, peeled, and sliced
6 large eggs, beaten
2 tablespoons chopped fresh cilantro
Yogurt and salsa

Preheat oven to 325°F. Spread tortilla strips in bottom of a generously greased 9- × -13-inch baking dish. Spread cheese over tortillas. Spread chilies over cheese. Combine eggs and cilantro and pour over chilies. Let sit for 5 minutes, then bake until set, about 20 to 25 minutes. Cool slightly, slice into squares, and serve with a dollop of yogurt and/or salsa. Try the Salsa Verde (page 134) with this dish.

Jalapeño-Stuffed Potatoes

 *4 servings*

Adjust the piquancy of these with more or less jalapeño or with a hotter or milder pepper.

4 large baking potatoes
½ cup light cream or milk
1 cup grated cheddar cheese
2 jalapeño peppers, chopped
1 teaspoon chili powder
½ teaspoon salt
¼ teaspoon black pepper
2 tablespoons minced fresh parsley

1. Preheat oven to 400°F. Pierce potatoes with a knife and bake until soft throughout, about 50 to 60 minutes. Remove and lower oven to 325°.

2. Let potatoes cool about 10 minutes, then slice the top third off. Scoop the flesh from the tops and the inside of the potatoes. Mash the flesh in a bowl with the cream or milk, ½ cup of the cheese, jalapeños, chili powder, salt, and pepper. Refill the potato shells. Bake for 25 minutes, remove, and turn on the broiler.

3. Sprinkle the remaining cheese over the tops and place under the broiler for about 1 minute, until the cheese is bubbling and browned. Sprinkle parsley over tops and serve hot.

Swordfish Veracruz

 *4 servings*

2 tablespoons olive oil
¾ cup sliced leeks
2 pounds Italian plum tomatoes, peeled, seeded, and coarsely
  chopped
3 chilies (poblanos, serranos, or jalapeños), seeded and chopped
1 tablespoon chopped fresh oregano
¼ cup chopped, pitted black olives
¼ cup dry white wine
4 8-ounce swordfish steaks
Salt and black pepper
2 tablespoons chopped fresh cilantro

1. Heat olive oil in a skillet and add leeks. Cook until soft, about 3 minutes.

2. Add tomatoes, chilies, oregano, olives, and wine and bring to a boil. Lower heat and simmer for about 20 minutes, while you prepare fish.

3. Brush fish lightly with additional olive oil. Broil just until fish is opaque and flakes easily.

4. Season sauce to taste with salt and pepper. Serve hot over fish, garnished with cilantro.

MUSHROOMS

One of the most intriguing group of "new" ingredients at the produce counter is the motley-looking (though sophisticate-priced) mushroom family. There are several thousand kinds of fungi, but only a few species are eaten. In America we accepted only one, the button or field mushroom, until recently. Now our evolving cuisine has given rise to a curiosity that allows the exotic species of France, Italy, China, and Japan to become household jargon.

What makes mushrooms so wonderful? No slouches in taste and aroma, they add a decidedly new dimension to any recipe—from a robust beefiness to a winelike tang or musky sweetness that is like that of no other food in the vegetable kingdom (though they are not really vegetables, reproducing by spores that are disseminated in the wind). The French, Italians, and other European and Asian cultures have known of their culinary value for ages. Soups, sauces, and meat dishes often take their character from a wild mushroom in these cuisines.

From April through November you will find several highly coveted varieties of fresh fungi, generally at the specialty produce stands, but more and more in the big supermarkets, too. The following lexicon will give you an idea of their differing idiosyn-crasies. Try them all.

Chanterelles (Cantharellus cibarius)   This wild mushroom cannot be cultivated, only gathered in the wild from our Pacific Northwest, the wettest area of temperate North America. Only the fresh chanterelles are worthy of your time and effort. The dried version are tough as rawhide and canned ones are insipid. Chanterelles are famous for their buttery texture, mildly apricot-spiced flavor, and idiosyncratic, nectarlike fragrance. They are available from mid-June through February, with summer and fall their peak seasons, and are much sturdier than other wild mushrooms. The peachy-fawn-colored mushroom's stem flares into the furled cap, sort of like a ridged trumpet. The flesh should feel firmly spongy, not waterlogged. You can store chanterelles for two days, wrapped in cloth or paper towel in the refrigerator. Brush or wipe off dirt with a damp towel and trim the ends. Slice, if desired. To enjoy them simply, cook them slowly over moderate heat for a few minutes until tender, but not browned and toughened, with garlic or shallots. The French give the *girolle*, as they also call the chanterelle, its culinary due. They let the sweetly aromatic mushrooms add depth to cream sauces, particularly those for fowl and game, as well as pasta, grain, and egg dishes.

Cloud Ears (Auricularia polytricha)   Also called *black mushrooms, black fungus, wood ears, tree ears, Judas' ear,* and *Jew's ear,* this fungus does resemble the ear with little stretch of the imagination. Cloud ears, a staple of Chinese cooking, have long been available in dried form but now you can very occasionally and very sporadically find them fresh. When soaked and rehydrated, the charcoal-black matter blossoms back to its suspended glutenous chewy texture. Mild tasting and chewy, cloud ears, called *kikurage* ("wood jellyfish") in Japanese, are used to add texture to stir-fries along with crunchy vegetables and meat or to cold vinaigrette salads. To rehydrate, cover the mushrooms with boiling water and allow them to soak for up to 30 minutes. The dried, petrified mushrooms keep almost forever, stored in a dark, dry spot.

Enoki (Flammulina velutipes)   The creamy white enoki (also called *enoki-dake, snow puff,* and *velvet stem*) looks more like a sprout than a mushroom. It is long and stringy with a tiny cap propped on its end. It is cultivated in sterilized organic material and is quite different from the wild mushroom from which it originates. Japan, California, and Malaysia all cultivate the neutral-flavored mushroom, which works best as a garnish, afloat in soups, dispersed in salads, or atop sandwiches. The enoki has little discernible flavor, so it is most renowned for its ornamental function and its crunchy texture. The lanky mushroom is available year round. It should be snowy white with no browning. Like a mass of sprouts, the joined bunch of mushrooms should not be too wet or slimy. Refrigerate them in their cellophane or plastic wrap. Mixed raw vegetable salads and thin but flavorful broths are good receptacles for enoki crunch. Do not cook the mushrooms much; add them raw to cold dishes or at the end of cooking for hot dishes.

Morels (Morchella conica, Morchella esculenta)   After truffles, morels are the most highly prized of fungi. They look something like a sea creature with their asparaguslike pointed heads pitted with spongelike caverns and their short stubby stems. The spongy ovals come in black and white (actually buff), the latter being more delicately flavored. The best commercially picked ones come from Wisconsin, Michigan, and elsewhere in the Midwest. The stems should not be shorter than 1 to 2 inches. Fresh ones should be moist and earthy, but firm and not too soiled. They'll keep in the refrigerator for up to 3 days, wrapped in paper towel. If particularly gritty, rinse quickly in a colander and pat dry with paper towel. Otherwise, simply brush or wipe clean with a damp towel. Then trim stem ends just before preparing. Sauté, braise, or simmer in cream. Add the cooked mushrooms to omelets, pasta, or grain dishes.

Dried morels are richer, more intense, and smokier than the fresh. They should have a strong woodsy flavor, but not a "fire

The Care and Handling of Mushrooms

COMMON NAMES	LATIN NAME	PEAK SEASON	AVAILABLE FORMS	LOOK FOR*	CLEANING AND STORAGE*
Chanterelle, girolle, egg mushroom	*Cantharellus cibarius*	Summer and fall	Wild only; fresh, canned, and dried	Firm, spongy texture; not too wet	Brush or wipe off dirt gently; store in refrigerator; use within 2 days.
Cloud ears, black mushrooms, wood ears, black fungus, Judas' ear, tree ears, Jew's ear	*Auricularia polytricha*	Year round	Cultivated only; mostly dried, occasionally fresh	Purplish-brown wrinkled clumps with moist, jellylike feel	No cleaning needed; trim bottom of cluster; store in refrigerator for up to 1 week.
Enoki, enoki-dake, snow puff, velvet stem	*Flammulina velutipes*	Year round	Cultivated only	Snowy white caps, no browning	No cleaning; store in refrigerator up to 3 days.
Morel, sponge mushroom	*Morchella conica, Morchella esculenta*	Spring and fall	Wild only; fresh and dried	Moist, spongy caps, heavy for size	Brush or wipe outside and inside when sliced; store in refrigerator, use quickly.
Porcini, cèpe, King Bolete, steinpilz, Polish mushroom	*Boletus edulis*	Summer and fall	Wild only; fresh and dried	Firm, springy texture	Brush or wipe gently; do not store unless absolutely necessary.
Shiitake, black forest mushroom, tung ku	*Lentinus edodes*	Year round	Occasionally wild, mostly cultivated; fresh and dried	Fresh pine scent, even color, and firm, evenly gilled caps	Brush or wipe, if dirty; refrigerate up to 3 days.
Truffles	*Tuber magnatum, Tuber melanosporum*	Late fall for white; winter for black	Wild only	Plump, firm, with dusky surface	Brush; refrigerate for up to 1 week

*These columns describe fresh mushrooms only.

sale" odor. A mycologist told me the latter odor indicates the mushrooms have been dried over dung fires in India or Afghanistan. The dried ones rehydrate quickly in a few minutes in water or stock. Cut off any tough ends, then slice lengthwise and rinse well to remove any remaining grit. I have found the richly pungent dried morels add great depth and complexity to a fresh tomato sauce. Even the addition of sweet peppers did not obscure their meaty, almost baconlike, flavor.

Porcini (Boletus edulis)   Also called *cèpes, steinpilz, Polish mushrooms,* or *King Bolete,* porcini (the name indicates "pigs' mushrooms" because pigs love the flavor) are a prized delicacy in Italy. Their availability in the fresh state is limited by a short growing season and high perishability. These meaty mushrooms, which appear in summer and autumn, are usually found in the Rockies, but also in cool moist areas near conifers and broadleaf trees. They have rust-brown caps and plump beige stems that flare at the base. They may also be pale or almost white if they were growing in a particularly dark part of the forest. Good ones should resist a firm squeeze and when sliced should be springy but not stringy. Their satin texture and sweet taste when fresh are so ephemeral that they should be savored at once. A simple quick sautéing in butter, olive oil, or a little of both until just golden will bring forth their taste at its peak. Fresh ones need cleaning with a damp cloth or a gentle brushing. Trim the tough stem end. The fresh porcini respond well to seasonings such as garlic, shallots, parsley, basil, tarragon, lemon, salt, and pepper. A spicy tomato sauce would mask their delicate flavor. But such is not the case with the dried version.

Dried porcini are easier to find year round, and though their character changes, they still have a wonderful pine-boskiness. The dried porcini look like dark or light (more expensive) gnarled twigs. They should not look too dark and hard. A 15- to 30-minute bath in water or stock rehydrates the dried mushroom. Always reserve the steeping liquid, which you must strain through several layers of cheesecloth or a coffee filter to remove grit. If the recipe doesn't call for the liquid (which some claim has more intense flavor than the soaked mushrooms), add it to soups, sauces, or stews. Rinse the revived mushrooms well in a colander to remove any remaining dirt or tiny pebbles. You can slice the mushrooms or leave them whole and add to soups, sauces, or gravies. Their smoky, earthy flavor will hold up and even develop with long cooking. Dried porcini keep indefinitely in your pantry.

Shiitake (Lentinus edodes) These sweet, robust, chewy mushrooms contain vitamins D, B_2, and B_{12} and are popular in Japanese cuisine. Also a popular ingredient in macrobiotic cooking, shiitake have been available for some time in health-food stores, generally in dried form. The fresh ones range from 2 to 9 inches in diameter. Fresh and dried forms are both good. The fresh ones should look firm but not be leathery and should have a pine forest scent. Size is not an indication of goodness, but since the cap is tender and the stem tough and fibrous, look for more cap than stem. The stems can be used to add flavor to a dish and then be discarded. These mushrooms are available year round in most areas, because they are widely cultivated.

Clean the caps with a damp cloth or brush to remove surface dirt and trim the stem ends. Slice the caps or leave them whole and savor sautéed with a drop of oil or butter and a splash of wine to develop their full range of goodness. Rejuvenate the dried mushrooms in water or stock until soft, about 20 to 30 minutes. Add them to soups, sauces, stir-fries, or vegetable and fish dishes.

Truffles These are mushrooms that produce their fruiting bodies underground in a symbiotic relationship with trees such as the oak, hazelnut, beech, and willow. Truffles are the total province of nature's whims. No science has been able to deliberately reproduce them. Specially trained dogs and pigs help truffle hunters find their black or white treasure. There may be well over 125 varieties of truffles found in the United States, but virtually none of them is worth eating. The most widely known truffles are the white or Alba truffle (*Tuber magnatum*), found only in Italy, in Piedmont and near the Apennines, and the black truffle (*Tuber melanosporum*) found in France, known as the *truffe de Périgord*.

The white truffle is considered the choicest of truffles and is prized for its perfume and flavor. It is in season in late fall. The white truffle is mildly redolent of raw garlic, and can be savored raw, thin slices lavished upon risotto, pasta, eggs, or meat dishes. The black truffle, which is in season in winter, must be cooked to develop its charm. It is good with cheese, butter, basil, and oregano. Truffle slices often flavor exquisite pâtés. The subterranean fungus should be sliced very thin, as its aroma is powerful.

Fresh truffles should feel plump and firm and have a dusky surface that is neither soft nor hard, nor rotting from moisture. Never wash or peel truffles. Brush them to remove dirt, then slice. They are perishable, but should keep for up to a week in the refrigerator.

Chanterelles, Arugula, and Toasted Walnut Salad

 *4 servings*

This deceptively simple combination is a medley of surprisingly lively and compatible flavors and textures. Serve as an appetizer or end-of-meal salad.

2 tablespoons butter
½ pound fresh chanterelles, cleaned and sliced
6 cups cleaned arugula
½ cup walnut halves, toasted
¼ cup fresh lemon juice
½ cup olive oil
Freshly ground pepper

1. Melt butter in a skillet. Add chanterelles and cook over moderately high heat, stirring frequently. Cook just until mushrooms are lightly golden, about 3 to 5 minutes. Set aside.

2. Arrange arugula, walnuts, and mushrooms on 4 salad plates. Combine lemon juice and olive oil and distribute over salads. Sprinkle on pepper and serve.

Enoki Broiled Cheddar Sandwiches with Spicy Dressing

 *4 servings*

The low-key enoki give the sandwich a nice succulent crunch and go very well with the cheddar and spicy sauce.

½ pound enoki mushrooms
8 slices whole-grain bread
4 large tomato slices
4 thick slices sharp cheddar cheese

Sauce
½ cup yogurt
¼ cup sour cream
2 tablespoons tomato paste or sauce
1 tablespoon whole-grain mustard
2 tablespoons peanut oil
¼ teaspoon sugar
Dash cayenne pepper

1. Distribute mushrooms over 4 slices of bread. Add tomato slices and cheese. Place under broiler until cheese is melted and bubbly.
2. Meanwhile, combine all sauce ingredients and mix well. Pour some dressing over each sandwich, cover with remaining bread slices, and serve.

Morels and Pasta

 *4 to 6 servings*

This is a classic worth repeating.

1 tablespoon butter
2 small shallots, finely minced
½ cup heavy cream
1 cup half-and-half
½ pound fresh morels, cleaned and sliced
¼ cup chopped fresh chervil
Salt and pepper to taste
1 pound fresh fettuccine, cooked

1. Melt butter in a saucepan, add shallots, and cook until soft, about 3 minutes. Stir in cream and half-and-half and simmer over low heat about 7 minutes, until slightly thickened.

2. Stir in morels and simmer another 7 minutes, until morels are slightly tender. Stir in chervil and season to taste. Toss sauce with cooked pasta and serve immediately.

Note: This sauce also goes well with chicken breasts or mild white fish.

Porcini and Pepper Tomato Sauce

 *Makes about 1½ quarts*

This spicy sauce is robust with the combination of the porcini and the peppers. The yield is more than enough for 1 pound of pasta. The leftover sauce keeps well for a few days or you can freeze it.

2 cups dried porcini
¼ cup olive oil

3 sweet yellow peppers, sliced into ½-inch strips
3 sweet red peppers, sliced into ½-inch strips
8 medium-size ripe tomatoes, peeled and chopped (about 5 to 6 cups)
2 teaspoons dried oregano
1 teaspoon dried thyme
½ teaspoon salt
¼ teaspoon crushed red pepper
¼ cup dry white wine

1. Combine the porcini and enough water to cover in a bowl. Set aside.

2. Heat olive oil in a large (4-quart) pot. Stir in red and yellow sweet peppers and cook over moderately high heat for about 7 minutes, until softened. Stir in tomatoes. Allow sauce to simmer over low heat for 30 to 45 minutes, until sauce begins to thicken.

3. Meanwhile, strain porcini, reserving 1 cup of liquid. Strain liquid through cheesecloth, and stir into cooking sauce. Chop mushrooms into smaller pieces and add to sauce. Add remaining ingredients and cook until sauce is thickened again, about 20 minutes. Serve over hot spaghetti, fettuccine, cappelli d'angeli, or other long, thin pasta.

Shiitake-Leek Monkfish

 *4 servings*

The firm-fleshed monkfish is a good match for meaty shiitake. Serve this dish accompanied by steamed rice.

2 thin strips bacon, diced
1 medium-sized leek, cleaned and sliced
½ pound fresh shiitake, cleaned and sliced
½ cup white stock

¼ cup dry white wine
1 tablespoon soy sauce
1 carrot
1 rib celery
1 small onion
¼ cup white wine vinegar
4 black peppercorns
2 pounds monkfish
Chopped fresh parsley
Freshly ground pepper

1. Sauté bacon in a skillet for about 3 minutes, until some fat is rendered. Add leeks and cook until soft. Stir in mushrooms and sauté gently for about 3 minutes. Stir in stock, wine, and soy sauce, and cook about another 5 minutes, stirring constantly. Cover and set aside to keep warm.

2. *Prepare fish:* Combine carrot, celery, onion, vinegar, and peppercorns in a saucepan with 4 cups of water. Bring to a boil. Lower in monkfish, and simmer for 8 to 10 minutes, until fish is just cooked through. Drain fish and cover with shiitake-leek mixture. Sprinkle with parsley and pepper. Serve immediately.

GRAINS, BEANS, NUTS, and SEEDS

Fruits and vegetables aren't the only categories of ingredients with items that are new to American cuisine. The following goods, including grains, flours, beans, and a few nuts, are staples in many foreign kitchens. For example, pine nuts, semolina flour, and fava beans are common foodstuffs in Italian kitchens, while few Middle Eastern homes would be without bulgur. The soy foods discussed here are as prevalent in the East as hamburgers in the West. These ingredients are now finding space in the American pantry and larder. You've tasted these foods in restaurants and your favorite chefs cook with them. Here's what you need to know to make them part of your own cooking repertoire.

GRAINS

Arborio Rice

Arborio rice is a special short-grain rice used to make the creamy *risotto alla milanese* and its manifold variations. Arborio is cultivated in the Po Valley in northern Italy. The grains of arborio are short and plump with a pearly translucency that cooks to a more glutenous *al dente* texture than our long- and short-grain white rice. The separate, drier texture of long-grain rice does not a proper risotto make. The cooking method and the proportion of liquid to rice is different. To make a basic risotto, the rice is coated in melted butter (with or without onions). A bouillon is then stirred in ladle by ladle as the grains slowly simmer. The rice absorbs more liquid this way—up to three times its uncooked volume. The constant stirring, along with the slowly incorporated stock, makes the risotto creamy and chewy, not dry and fluffy. Just before serving, the steaming rice is finished with a swift whipping in of butter and Parmesan cheese. Classic additions to this northern Italian dish include spices, wine, and minced vegetables. Arborio is available in Italian food markets. Store it as you would other rice—away from heat, light, and moisture.

Risotto with Porcini

 *4 to 6 servings*

This creamy but chewy rice dish requires constant vigilance but is well worth the effort.

4 tablespoons butter
2 small shallots, finely minced
1/2 pound fresh porcini, cleaned and chopped
2 cups arborio rice
1 cup dry white wine
6 cups chicken stock
1/2 cup Parmesan cheese
Chopped fresh basil

1. Melt 2 tablespoons of butter in a large saucepan, add shallots and porcini, and cook 3 minutes.

2. Stir in rice with a wooden spoon to coat evenly with butter. Cook 3 minutes, stirring constantly.

3. Stir in wine and about 1 cup of stock. Continue to stir constantly, adding stock cup by cup for about 20 minutes so that rice absorbs liquid and does not stick to pan.

4. Remove from heat, cover, and let sit for 5 minutes. Whip in remaining butter and Parmesan. Stir in basil and serve.

Basmati Rice

Basmati rice is a popular variety of rice grown and used frequently in India, where as much as one-third of the arable land is given to the cultivation of this vital grain. Basmati is a long-grain rice with a pleasant musky flavor and aroma that is well suited to spicy Indian cooking. As a long-grain rice, basmati is richer in the starch amylose, which helps render a dry, fluffy, cooked product that Indian cooks desire for the many and varied rice dishes they prepare. The shorter grain rices, on the other hand, are higher in the starch amylopectin, which is responsible for the creamier glutenous quality of rice such as arborio (page 155). Basmati is available in Indian food stores and in some supermarkets.

Spiced Rice and Peas

 *4 servings*

3 tablespoons butter
¾ cup minced onions
1 tablespoon Garam Masala (see page 201)

2 cups basmati rice
4½ cups water
½ teaspoon salt
2 cups fresh peas
1 large clove garlic, minced

Melt the butter and sauté the onions until they begin to brown. Stir in the Garam Masala, and cook another minute. Stir in rice and add water, salt, peas, and garlic. Bring to a boil, reduce heat to low, cover, and simmer until water is absorbed, about 20 minutes.

Blue Cornmeal

The Pueblo Indians of Arizona and New Mexico have long considered blue corn an important starch in their diet. Actually the ears of corn are deep slate-blue with varying shades of grayish-lavender and purple. The centuries-old grain is still cultivated in the Southwest. The Indians parched, cracked, and ground the corn to make various types of dense breads, including the still-popular tortilla flatbread. That is pretty much how the blue corn is still treated today, minus the pomp and ceremony that the Indians invested in preparation of their life-sustaining crop. The Indians also roast and thicken blue corn flour (called *atole*) with milk or water into a hot, rib-sticking porridge.

Unless its outer-space color bothers you, blue cornmeal is virtually interchangeable with white and yellow cornmeal. Some slight differences may be of interest to certain cooks: White cornmeal has a rougher texture than yellow, and blue is the finest of all three. Due to its softer endosperm (the heart of the grain), the blue corn is closer to the smooth texture of a flour when ground than to that of grainy cornmeal. Blue corn is not a hybrid, it is open-pollinated, meaning it will self-reproduce, this being of interest to purists who object to the slightest tampering with nature. On a par nutritionally with white and yellow cornmeal, blue cornmeal may be slightly higher in manganese and a couple of other trace minerals.

Tastewise, you may notice no difference or a slightly more pronounced flavor when blue cornmeal is used. Use the blue just about anywhere you'd use white or yellow—in mush, Johnnycakes, hotcakes, waffles, quickbreads, or yeast breads. One application in which you don't want to use blue cornmeal is polenta. Stick to the traditional grainy yellow one for this Italian peasant "bread." Blue cornmeal gives baked goods an earthy blue-gray cast, similar to the color buckwheat imparts to foods.

A few years ago, unless you lived in the heart of the Southwest, it was almost certain you'd have to get your blue cornmeal via mail order. But now the health-foods business promotes this high-carbohydrate's nutrition, and the preoccupation with regional cuisine also supports its wider availability. Arrowhead Mills (which grows its own blue corn) in Hereford, Texas, and other natural-foods manufacturers distribute blue cornmeal throughout the country to health-food stores. It is more expensive than other cornmeal due to tedious cultivation methods and a lower crop yield.

Store blue cornmeal in tightly sealed plastic or glass containers away from heat and light. The ideal spot is in the freezer, where it will keep for a year or longer. If you store it at room temperature, make sure it's not easy prey for migrant insects; use it (and all grains) within three months.

Blue Cornmeal Apple Pancakes

 *4 servings*

1½ cups blue cornmeal
½ cup unbleached white flour
1 teaspoon baking powder
1 teaspoon baking soda
½ teaspoon salt
2 eggs
2 tablespoons honey
1½ cups buttermilk
2 tablespoons vegetable oil
2 baking apples, peeled, cored, and thinly sliced

1. Combine all dry ingredients in a mixing bowl. In another bowl, beat eggs, honey, buttermilk, and oil together. Stir dry ingredients into wet. Stir in apples.

2. Prepare a lightly oiled griddle. Pour pancakes to desired size and cook until lightly browned on each side. Serve with butter and syrup, jam, or cinnamon sugar.

Bulgur

Though its name is an exotic Middle Eastern word, bulgur comes from the grain with which Americans are most at home, wheat. However, while our industrialized country has generally taken the amber waves of grain through high-speed milling to the wonder of airy bread, Middle Eastern cuisine has applied only low technology to the wheat grain. The whole wheat berry, as the grain is called, is simply cracked between rollers into four to six pieces. Bulgur (or *bulgar*, *burghul*, and various similar spellings) is cracked wheat that has been hulled and parboiled in a way that preserves most of the nutrients, but also greatly reduces cooking time—from over an hour to about 15 minutes. Syrians and Lebanese use bulgur, ground to specified fine and coarse textures, to make the ever-popular tabbouleh (a refreshing summer salad, savory with a fresh mint, lemon juice, and olive oil dressing) and kibbeh (wheat and ground beef or lamb). The coarser bulgur is often used in pilafs, in casseroles, soups, and stews.

Bulgur, most often found in natural-foods stores, has the nutty sweet taste of wheat and is a wonderful change from rice and potato side dishes. It is extremely versatile and, because it contains the fiber and nutrient-rich bran and germ, it is most nourishing. Tan-and-cream-colored bulgur looks wholesome, but you may want to enliven its appearance and taste with some colorful red peppers, broccoli florets, carrot slices, or snow peas, all perfect taste and texture blends.

To cook bulgur: Bring 2 cups of water for every cup of grain to a boil. Stir in grain, turn heat down to low, cover, and simmer (no stirring) about 15 minutes, or until all the liquid is absorbed. Season with butter and salt, if desired, and serve hot.

Refrigerate bulgur, if space permits, or store it at room temperature in a cool dark place, tightly sealed in plastic or glass. The partially cooked grain keeps fairly well at room temperature, but use it within three months.

Sage-Nut Bulgur Pilaf

 *6 servings*

2 tablespoons butter
¼ cup chopped onion
1½ cups bulgur

¼ cup pine nuts
¼ cup chopped walnuts
¼ cup chopped toasted almonds
¼ teaspoon cinnamon
½ teaspoon grated orange zest
2 cups stock
½ teaspoon salt
¼ cup chopped fresh sage

Melt butter in a large skillet and sauté onion for 3 minutes. Stir in bulgur, nuts, cinnamon, and zest. Add stock and salt. Stir once, cover, and simmer until water is absorbed, about 15 to 20 minutes. Stir in sage and serve hot.

Gluten Flour

Gluten is the protein substance in flours, most notably in wheat, that allows bread and baked goods to rise. Gluten flour derives from wheat flour that has had some of its starch content removed, so as to concentrate the protein until the flour is about three-quarters gluten. Gluten may be added to yeasted bread-dough mixtures for one of two reasons: to increase the protein content or to raise the bread more effectively (especially if dense, low-gluten whole grains are used). If you read ingredient lists on commercially baked whole-grain breads, you'll see how commonly gluten flour is added.

Kneading bread develops the gluten and as the yeast organisms expel their gases into the dough, the resilient elastic protein substance expands like many tiny balloons being filled with air. You can produce gluten at home by forming a ball of dough from flour and water and kneading it under water until the starch washes out. The sticky, chewy substance that remains is of interest to certain vegetarian regimes. Called *seitan*, it is marinated with soy sauce and spices and served as a meat substitute for the vegetarian who needs one.

You'll find gluten flour in specialty-food stores and sometimes in natural-foods stores. Store it away from heat and light in an airtight plastic or glass container and use within six months.

Graham Flour

Graham is simply another name for whole wheat flour, named after the nineteenth-century reverend Sylvester Graham. Graham was a New England minister who bemoaned the way high-speed milling neutered the wheat grain into a lifeless white powder. The Reverend Graham was a strong and vociferous advocate of whole unmilled grain, which retains its fibrous bran and nutrient-rich germ. Graham would no doubt be pleased to see that that fiber is at last seeing its day as a salubrious foodstuff. Whole wheat baked goods are very much appreciated now for their old-fashioned nutty flavor.

Use whole wheat flour in any recipe calling for graham flour. Some manufacturers may distinguish a coarser ground whole wheat flour as graham, but this should be noted on the package. If you have thought that whole wheat tastes like cardboard, it is probably because you've only tasted products made with whole wheat flour that was slightly rancid, an easy occurrence. Unlike white flour, whole wheat turns quickly, thanks to the oily germ portion, which also attracts bugs more easily. So store whole wheat flour in the freezer and use it within three to six months to enjoy its full nutty flavor.

Kasha (Buckwheat)

Kasha is actually an Eastern European cracked meal made from buckwheat, the grain from which the dark, richly flavored hotcakes of southern breakfast fame are made. Buckwheat is always hulled and cracked into kasha or ground into flour. This pseudo-grain has Old World roots. Steaming plates of *kasha varnishkes* stir up feelings of nostalgia for anyone of Ukrainian or Eastern European ancestry.

Although buckwheat is botanically a fruit, related to rhubarb, dock, and sorrel, it is treated like a grain and can be used just about any way grain is—in pilafs, stuffings, soups, stews, and casseroles. Toasted buckwheat, cooked in water until swollen and tender, then served with butter or gravy, makes a good side dish to beef, pork, liver, or lamb.

Buckwheat has high-quality protein, a good amount of B vitamins and iron and calcium. It is available roasted (called kasha) or unroasted. The roasting deepens the special flavor, aroma, and color of wholesome buckwheat. It is sold in fine, medium, and coarse textures, the finer ones cooking the fastest. Store buckwheat away from light and heat, preferably in the freezer or refrigerator in airtight containers.

Kasha, Mushrooms, and Roasted Eggplant

 *4 servings*

1 medium-size eggplant
Olive oil
2 tablespoons butter

½ pound button mushrooms, cleaned and sliced
1 cup coarse kasha
1 egg
2 cups boiling meat or vegetable stock
½ teaspoon salt

1. Preheat oven to 400°F. Wash but do not peel eggplant (unless it is aged and the skin seems as if it may be bitter and tough). Slice into ¾-inch rounds. Brush both sides lightly with olive oil, then quarter the rounds into wedges. Place on a baking sheet and bake until eggplant is soft through, turning over once, about 10 to 15 minutes.

2. Meanwhile, prepare kasha. Melt butter in a heavy-bottom skillet. Add mushrooms and sauté for 3 minutes. Mix kasha with egg. Stir into mushrooms for 2 to 3 minutes.

3. Stir in boiling stock, cover skillet, lower heat, and simmer for 5 minutes, until liquid is absorbed.

4. Fluff grains, toss gently with roasted eggplant, add salt, and serve as a side dish.

Masa Harina

Masa harina is finely ground flour made from whole hominy, also known as *mote*, *pozole*, and *nixtamal*. Hominy is whole corn that is processed by soaking the corn with lime, calcium carbonate, lye, or wood ash to loosen the hulls. The corn is then separated from the hulls, washed, and dried—and ready to impart the distinct corn flavor to the renowned Mexican flatbreads once it is ground.

The word *masa* means "dough" in Spanish and refers to the corn dough used in the making of tortillas, tamales, and enchiladas. The specially ground flour can also be used for other Mexican and South American corn recipes. Quaker Oats distributes the product under the trade name Masa Harina. Masa harina is the only flour that can turn out a proper tortilla, with the right taste and texture. You can find this special flour in Mexican or Spanish grocery stores.

Store masa harina as you would all flours—in airtight plastic or glass away from heat, moisture, and light, and use within three months.

Tortillas

 *Makes 12 tortillas*

This recipe is taken from *Creative Cooking with Grains and Pasta*, by Mel and Sheryl London (Emmaus, Penn.: Rodale Press, 1984).

2 cups masa harina
1¼ cups warm water

1. Place masa harina in a mixing bowl and gradually add the warm water, blending with a wooden spoon. Use hands to knead dough until smooth (about 3 to 4 minutes). Divide dough into 12 walnut-size balls, place in a bowl, and cover with a towel or aluminum foil. Let stand for about 5 minutes. When making each tortilla, keep remainder of dough covered so that it doesn't dry out.

2. Heat a heavy iron skillet, griddle, or *comal* (a Mexican version) over medium-high heat. Flatten each ball by patting it two or three times between the palms of your hands and place the dough on a tortilla press with a piece of plastic or a small plastic food storage bag (6¾ inches x 8¼ inches) placed on the bottom plate. Cover dough with a second plastic bag. Close the lid and press just hard enough to flatten the dough. (Dough should be

placed closer to the top of the press to make a perfect circle when pressure is applied.) Open press and peel top plastic off slowly, being careful not to break the thin circle. Then lift the entire bottom piece of plastic along with the tortilla off the press and turn it upside down on the first piece of plastic. Then peel the second piece off slowly. Lift tortilla with plastic and turn it off the plastic gently and onto the ungreased hot skillet. Cook for about 30 seconds. The edges should look dry and the underside will be speckled with brown. Turn with a spatula and bake for 1 minute, then turn back to the first side and bake another 30 seconds. The tortilla will puff up. Wrap in foil, or a towel or napkin, to keep warm and soft. After you make each tortilla, add it to the pile in the towel and cover.

Note: The plastic should peel off easily once you get the knack. If it seems too dry, add more water to the dough. If the plastic sticks, add more masa harina.

You can freeze tortillas for several weeks. When you're ready to use them, just reheat them in a slow oven.

Millet

Although it is most often embedded in suet globes and fed to the birds, millet is a most nutritious member of the grain family, easily digested, rich in good protein, B vitamins, and iron. If you've ever eaten in an Ethiopian restaurant, you have surely savored the national bread, called *injera*, a flat bread made from millet and used as a scoop for all the lively dishes served there. In northern Africa millet is also cooked into a porridge called *tuo zaafi*, and in Central Africa, a small, flat bread called *taguella*.

Stocked for years as an offbeat health food, along with other whole grains, millet has more and more mainstream interest now. It is indeed one of the milder flavored grains, but as our concern for eating a higher carbohydrate diet grows, millet is coming out of the closet, showing its versatility in the kitchen. It is fairly quick-cooking—25 to 30 minutes of boiling. It is easily prepared as a simple side dish with butter and salt or in more creative fashion with a colorful array of vegetables and cheese, as a pilaf, a stuffing, in soups, stews, or casseroles.

Millet makes a good dessert grain, baked into an almond- or vanilla-flavored pudding or sweetened and mixed with fresh fruit. It makes a delicious salutary hot breakfast cereal mixed with nuts or seeds, dried fruit, and maple syrup or honey. Mix millet with oats, rice, or any of the other grains for pleasant taste and textural contrasts. Cooked millet is very similar to egg-rich pastina—tiny balls of dough cooked with egg and butter, often appealing to children.

Presently, the most surefire place to find millet is in a natural-foods store. Store the grain away from heat and light in an airtight container.

Chili con Carne and Millet

 *4 to 6 servings*

5 cups water
½ teaspoon salt
2 cups millet
1 tablespoon butter

For the chili con carne
2 pounds ground beef chuck or round
1 large onion, chopped
1 large green pepper, seeded and chopped
2 chilies (jalapeños or serranos), seeded and chopped

3 cloves garlic, minced
2 cups chopped tomatoes
1 cup tomato puree
1 tablespoon chili powder
1 teaspoon ground cumin
1½ cups cooked kidney beans

1. Bring water and salt to a boil in saucepan. Stir in millet, lower to simmer, and cook until liquid is absorbed, about 25 minutes, then add butter.

2. Meanwhile, cook chili. Heat beef, onion, pepper, chilies, and garlic in a heavy skillet until beef is browned.

3. Stir in tomatoes, puree, chili powder, and cumin. Simmer, partially covered, another 45 minutes. Stir in beans and simmer until heated through. Serve on a bed of steaming millet.

Quinoa

It's earthy and ancient—over three thousand years old. The Incas valued it highly, calling it the "mother" grain. As amaranth (see page 55) was to the Aztecs, so quinoa ("KEEN-wah" or "keen-NO-wah") was to the Incas, a grain worthy of the most sacred ritual. Today, both grains are available in this country thanks to the renewed fervor of a few moderns. The Quinoa Corporation, started in the early eighties by two entrepreneurs, Steve Gorad and Don McKinley, imports and distributes most of the quinoa in this country.

Higher in protein, calcium, and iron than other grains, quinoa's nutritive values are of great interest to food researchers in this country. Quinoa is notably high in three amino acids—lysine, methionine, and cystine—a particularly beneficial combination of protein building blocks for a grain.

Although quinoa is found most easily in health-food stores, the grain is attracting an upscale market and can now be found in gourmet food stores as well. At this writing, quinoa ranges in price from $1.84 to $3.20 per pound.

The disk-shaped grains are sand-colored and, except for a slight grayish cast, look like millet. Each grain has a flattened band, actually the germ, around its girth. As the grains puff up with cooking, the bands detach and resemble little sprouts. Cooked quinoa is easily mistaken for sprouted millet. It cooks up quickly— in about 15 minutes—to a very tender consistency. The mild, ricelike taste is a perfect foil for emphatic seasonings such as curries, chilies, or tomato-based toppings. Cook quinoa in a mild stock instead of water for a flavorful variation.

Use quinoa as you would any other grain. I've enjoyed this versatile grain in a chicken soup, in a Mexican platter with a red chili sauce and yucca, as a refreshing cold salad with scallions and sesame seeds, and in a couscous preparation (recipe follows).

Quinoa Couscous with Rabbit Stew

 *4 to 6 servings*

¼ cup olive oil
2¾ to 3 pounds rabbit, cut into pieces
3 to 4 cloves garlic, chopped
3 cups canned tomatoes, slightly mashed
3½ cups chicken stock
½ teaspoon ground coriander
¼ teaspoon ground ginger
¼ teaspoon ground cumin
¼ teaspoon cinnamon
¼ teaspoon cayenne pepper

½ teaspoon salt
3 carrots, cut into ½-inch slices
2 cups cooked chick-peas
2 cups quinoa
¾ pound mushrooms, sliced

1. In a large skillet, heat oil and add rabbit. Cook over moderately high heat, turning pieces until nicely browned.
2. Remove rabbit with a slotted spoon to a 4-quart pot. Set skillet with oil and meat juices aside. Add garlic, tomatoes, stock, coriander, ginger, cumin, cinnamon, cayenne, and salt to rabbit. Cook uncovered over moderate heat for 1½ hours, stirring occasionally.
3. Add carrots to pot, cover, and cook another 30 to 45 minutes, until carrots are tender. Stir in chick-peas.
4. While carrots are cooking, prepare quinoa: Combine quinoa with 6 cups cold water in a pot with a tight-fitting lid. Bring to a boil, lower heat, and simmer until all water is absorbed, about 15 minutes.
5. Heat reserved oil and meat juices in skillet and add mushrooms. Cook until browned, about 7 minutes. To serve, ladle rabbit stew over quinoa; top with mushrooms.

Semolina

Semolina is the most popular flour used to make sturdy pasta—with or without eggs. This sunny-yellow flour, the texture of fine cornmeal, is ground from the heart, or *endosperm*, of a hard wheat called *durum*. The coarse flour is very practical for pasta-making as it yields noodles that hold their own through the rigors of shaping, drying, cooking, and in reaching that elusive *al dente* state. You can use all or part semolina flour in making pasta, for variations in texture. Semolina is ideal for the dumplinglike gnocchi, which will not have the right chewiness without some semolina added to the potato dough.

Semolina is also used in baked goods—cakes, puddings, and sweet dumplings. It is the grain that is used to make the popular North African stew couscous. The coarse flour is rubbed and worked through a sieve by hand until it forms the right texture for the spicy meat and vegetable concoction.

Because it is lacking in the oil-rich germ and bran, semolina flour stores well at room temperature, but do use it within six months for optimum flavor. Store it away from heat and light in an airtight container.

Semolina Egg Pasta

 *Makes 1 pound*

2 cups semolina flour
½ teaspoon salt (optional)
2 large eggs
2 tablespoons olive oil

1. Place flour and salt, if desired, in work bowl of food processor fitted with metal blade. With machine on, add eggs, then oil through the feed tube. Process for about 1 minute past the point where dough adheres in a ball. If dough is too dry, add a little more oil or another egg. If too wet, add more flour. If the dough is the right moisture, but still doesn't quite adhere in a ball, stop the machine and work the pieces into a ball with your hands. Set the dough aside to rest under a damp towel.

2. Prepare pasta machine. Divide dough into 6 balls, leaving them under the damp towel until you're ready for them. Roll dough into sheets, starting with the widest setting, working the dough

down to as thin as you like it (usually the second-to-last setting is thin enough). This helps knead the dough further. Set the strips aside on a clean towel or linen.

3. When all the dough is rolled into strips, start cutting it into the shape of pasta you want. By the time you are done cutting all the dough strips the pasta will have dried out enough for cooking. Or you can let it dry further for a few hours or overnight. If you decide to store it, freeze it in a cardboard box dusted with cornmeal. Cook directly from the freezer; do not thaw.

BEANS

Adzuki Beans

Adzuki beans are not well known in the United States, but they're as common in Japan, where they originated, as lima beans are in the U.S. In fact they are grown all over the Orient and are often paired in dishes with rice, a complementary protein. Sweet and tasty adzukis are small, cylindrical beans, red to maroon in color. They can be eaten whole, mashed, seasoned, or baked as patties.

At one time you could find adzuki beans only in the health-food store. But now, as our interest in ethnic and exotic fare grows, adzukis are easier to find in a supermarket with a wide bean selection or in Asian food shops.

Adzukis are a legume with a good quality protein, which can be added enticement to those who eat little or no meat. Like other dried beans, adzukis also contain iron and some B vitamins and plenty of fiber. If you prepare them as part of a meatless meal, be sure to include a grain, such as brown rice, bulgur (wheat), or millet to supply the amino acids (tryptophan) that adzukis are a little short on; adzukis can supply the lysine in which grains are deficient.

You must soak adzukis to rehydrate them before cooking as you would other dried beans, such as kidneys, pintos, and dried limas. Soak them for about 6 hours or overnight. Change the soak water as often as you like and reduce the beans' worrisome flatulence factor—but at the expense of some water-soluble vitamins. The beans cook in under an hour.

Use adzukis as you would other dried beans. They add taste, texture, and substance to vegetable soups or stews. With a zesty mustard or lemon vinaigrette they are good in salad, especially with fresh vegetables. They go well with beef, pork, lamb, chicken, or fish dishes.

I have found adzukis to be a good sprouting bean—a fun way to grow produce in your own kitchen, if you remember to rinse the sprouts a few times daily. (If you decide to sprout the beans, be sure to rehydrate them in water for 6 to 8 hours first.) The sprouts are as nutritious as the dried beans and add a nice crunch and sweetness to fresh salads.

Adzukis, like other dried beans, keep well for up to a year, if you protect them from sunlight, moisture, and air.

Adzuki and Squash

 *4 servings*

1 cup dried adzuki beans
1 1-pound ham bone
1½ cups diced butternut squash
1 cup sliced carrots
1 teaspoon curry powder
Salt and pepper to taste

1. Soak beans in about 5 cups of water in a large pot for at least 6 hours. Drain beans, add ham bone to pot, and cover with 4 cups water. Bring to a boil, reduce heat, and simmer for 1 hour.

2. Stir in squash, carrots, and curry powder and simmer 20 minutes longer. Add salt and pepper to taste. Serve hot with brown rice or other grain.

Carob

Also called *locust bean* or *St. John's bread*, carob appeared in the Bible long before it ever appeared in a cookbook. It was the food that once sustained John the Baptist. Carob, most often associated with health-food confections, is actually a legume growing inside long, leathery chocolate-brown pods in Mediterranean countries. The pods are a treat for little children in Italy, who enjoy sucking on them. Carob is available as a powder for baking and often as candy, looking very slyly like milk chocolate.

In fact, carob was once considered the miracle stand-in for chocolate, supposedly imparting the virtues of that addictive food minus the vices. Most chocoholics disagree vehemently, perceiving little likeness between the two. From a nutritional standpoint, carob does come out substantially ahead of cocoa, the nonvirtuous part of chocolate. Carob has roughly 50 calories per ounce, cocoa has 84. Carob is naturally about 50 percent sweeter than cocoa and has no caffeine, theobromine (another stimulant), or oxalic acid (which binds calcium), as does cocoa.

You would do much greater justice to chocolate and carob to think of them as two distinct foods, each with worthwhile culinary usage. Although carob is dark, brown, and chocolaty looking, it takes a commercial roasting process to make carob powder look anything like cocoa. Be aware that the powder can also turn to an unappealing charcoal gray when used for a beverage.

I have tried several carob cake recipes sweetened with honey. They were good, though I suspect that was largely due to the high butter content. The best thing I ever made with carob powder was crêpes. They were quite easy to make and had a very appetizing chocolate color. A tender texture and mild sweetness made them perfect wrapping for a walnut filling with whipped cream.

Although carob is most often used for sweet goods, try sifting some of the powder (actually flour) into bread dough for some surprisingly pleasant changes. Several years ago a health-food store in San Francisco supplied me regularly with a heavenly dense brown carob-dosed bread called St. John's. It was moist with a maltlike sweetness, and was ever so deliciously filling with melted Camembert and tomato.

I have found a recipe for making carob powder from the pods, which are available now, but all the time-consuming and tedious soaking, grinding, drying, and sifting hardly seem worth the inferior end product. Health-food stores supply a good quality product. Carob powder or flour keeps well in the freezer for a year or longer.

Carob Crêpes

 *Makes about 1 dozen*

Fill these with sweet nut, cream, or fruit fillings. Or, to use for savory fillings, omit the sugar.

3 large eggs
¼ cup melted butter
¾ cup milk
1 cup unbleached white flour
¼ cup carob powder
¼ teaspoon salt
1 tablespoon sugar

1. Beat eggs, butter, and milk together in a mixing bowl. Mix flour, carob, salt, and sugar in another bowl. Beat flour mixture

into wet ingredients until batter is evenly mixed. Refrigerate for 1 to 2 hours.

2. Heat a 6-inch crêpe pan and oil lightly. Pour in enough batter to coat pan when you tip it, about 1½ tablespoons. Cook about 1 minute, or until crêpe pulls away easily from pan. Flip and cook the other side briefly, about 30 seconds. Fill crêpes or wrap and freeze.

Cowpeas (Black–Eyed Peas)

Cowpeas, more familiarly known as *black-eyed peas*, are neither peas nor beans, but botanically are closer to the bean. Cowpea can actually refer to any number of species of the *Vigna* genus, which yields pods up to 12 inches long containing peas or beans varying from maroon to red, brown, black, pink, or white, solid or speckled. The fresh ones are generally called *peas* in the South, where they are most popular, and the dried bean of the black-eyed variety is designated *bean*. I use *cowpea* here to refer to the dried black-eyed pea.

The cowpea genus has been around for eons and the different varieties have a niche of sorts in many different cuisines. The bean made its way from the dawn of history through Arabia and Asia Minor and China. It has been an important food in India and Africa, too, used fresh or dried, its mild peanutty flavor a natural match for hot and spicy curry blends. Italians got wind of the beans in the fourteenth century and worked them into Mediterranean dishes. The pea-bean made it to this country around the eighteenth century as *pease*, *callicance*, or *cavalance* (from the West Indian name). Creole cooks found it quite useful. Black-eyed peas simmered with ham hock or bacon, rice, and hot pepper make the lively classic southern favorite Hoppin' John (see recipe following).

The creamy ovals with their gaping black-eye trademark can be used like other dried beans. They must be rehydrated, then simmered for about 1 hour until tender. They're good in soups with strong seasonings or in casseroles topped with cheese. They retain a firm texture when cooked and make a good cold salad ingredient, too. They are a good source of vegetable protein, especially when combined with rice or other grains. The dried black-eyed peas are easily available in most large supermarkets.

Hoppin' John

 — 6 to 8 servings

1½ cups cowpeas
1 cup chopped onions
½ cup chopped celery
¼ teaspoon crushed red pepper
2 bay leaves
½ pound chopped salt pork
1 cup uncooked rice

1. Soak cowpeas in 6 cups water for 6 hours or overnight. Drain and cover with 5 cups of water. Add onions, celery, pepper, and bay leaves. Bring to a boil, lower heat to simmer, and cook for 1 hour.

2. Stir in salt pork and rice and cook for another 25 to 30 minutes, until rice is tender. Correct seasoning and serve hot.

Cranberry Beans

Cranberry beans are one more ancient legume enjoying a renaissance today, dressed with sumptuous sauces, zestful vinaigrettes, or in heart- and soul-warming soups and stews. This cranberry-speckled bean is more visible now because, as with other dried beans, there is more interest in its fresh form. The dried bean has long been available and requires the usual soaking and hour or so of cooking, after which it can be channeled into all manner of meat or vegetable and bean dishes.

The fresh bean appears at market at the end of summer in a green pod dappled with pink. The plump two-toned white-and-red-spotted gems are easily shaken out. You can boil or steam the fresh beans in about 20 to 30 minutes. Then season simply or elaborately as you would other beans. Unfortunately, cooking robs the bean of its jewel-like façade, rendering it a uniformly dull pink. But these beans remain fairly firm and tasty with cooking. They have a chewy texture with a potato- and squashlike flavor. I find olive oil, balsamic vinegar, garlic, and Parmesan cheese to be a nice set of flavorings for the cooked fresh or dried beans. I add the leftover ones to pasta and tomato dishes for a good-quality protein blend and a tasty, satisfying meal. Do buy the cranberry beans fresh when available and use them within a few days.

Cranberry Beans au Gratin

 *4 servings*

2 cups cooked fresh or dried cranberry beans
½ cup heavy cream

²/₃ cup grated fontina cheese
¹/₄ cup Parmesan cheese
2 tablespoons fresh thyme, sage, basil, or rosemary
2 tablespoons butter
²/₃ cup bread crumbs
¹/₃ cup grated mozzarella cheese

1. Preheat oven to 350°F. Butter a 2-quart ovenproof casserole.
2. Combine beans, cream, fontina and Parmesan cheeses, and herb. Mix well and turn into prepared casserole.
3. Melt butter and combine with bread crumbs. Sprinkle over top of beans, and bake for 25 minutes. Sprinkle mozzarella over top of casserole and bake 5 minutes longer, until cheese is melted. Serve immediately.

Fava Beans

Also called *broad beans*, fava beans are available dried or fresh. And both versions have different appeal. The fava bean has a squat, flat kidney shape and is green when fresh, buff when dried. As with other dried beans, favas have loomed more prominently in the cuisine of other countries, most notably that of the Middle East, Mediterranean Europe, and Africa. In the Middle East the broad bean is often a substitute for the chick-pea, used whole or pureed and mixed with tahini and spices.

It is a mystery why the mild-flavored bean, tasting something like a cross between fried potato skins and raw peanuts, does not enjoy more esteem here. It is easy to grow and has noteworthy nutrients, including as much protein as fresh lima beans, plus more iron and potassium. It is a low-fat and high-carbohydrate food too, filling and versatile. Favas will no doubt gain wider acceptance as they become more available in the marketplace in fresh and dried form.

Available in the spring, fresh favas are a nice change from lima beans, and can be used in the same way. Remove the beans from their fat green pods. You can also simmer, steam, or sauté young favas in the pod or add the shelled beans to heartier fare with more assertive seasoning. Boil the larger favas in the pod, then shell and eat them when cooled, the way Italians do—as an appetizer, plain or with a sprinkling of oil and vinegar. Dried fava beans can be used in all these ways once they are rehydrated and cooked until tender, for about 1 hour. Roast the cooked beans like peanuts for a novel nutritious treat. Or do as the French do— puree the bean and enrich it with cream and seasonings to serve with meat.

When buying fresh favas, select plump, velvety pods that show no signs of shriveling or decay. Refrigerate and use them within a few days. Dried favas should look evenly tanned, be of uniform size, with smooth seed coats and no shriveling. Store these in airtight containers, away from heat, light, and moisture.

Baked Favas with Thyme

 *4 servings*

2 cups shelled favas
³/₄ cup heavy cream
¹/₄ teaspoon nutmeg
1 tablespoon chopped fresh thyme
¹/₂ cup grated Swiss cheese

Preheat oven to 350°F. Combine favas, cream, nutmeg, and thyme in a mixing bowl. Pour into a well-buttered baking dish.

Bake until favas are tender, about 20 minutes. Sprinkle cheese over top and bake another 5 to 10 minutes, until cheese is bubbly and brown. Serve hot.

Lupini Beans

If you are going to broaden your spectrum of dried beans you may as well at least sample lupini beans, which, like favas, have been available in Italian communities just about forever. They often appear on the hot and cold buffet table during the holidays, especially between Christmas and New Year's in Italian homes. But the humble legume is easily overshadowed amid a throng of other goodies—bowls of briny olives, marinated peppers and vegetables, breaded and fried fish, stuffed artichokes, and other festive fare. Lupini, like fresh stalks of fennel, are best suited to keeping your jaws busy while you await the return of appetite for the endless feast.

The tan beans are available in jars of brine or you can find them dried to cook on your own. They are wide yellowish full moons. To eat them requires an easily learned art. You slip the bean into your mouth, apply just enough pressure with your teeth to pierce the tough seed coat and deftly slip the crunchy, chewy bean into your mouth. Discard the translucent seed covering. It takes a little practice before you get it right. I first learned to eat lupini at the home of friends, the Romano family, in the heart of South Philly during New Year's festivities. My first attempt sent the buff-colored bean flying like a Frisbee into the platter of fried smelts in the center of the table. The Romano family and I will never forget the wrong way to extricate lupini.

Lupini are very mild flavored, requiring salt, pepper, and vinegar to bring some zip to them. Though I suppose they have wider culinary possibilities than just as an appetizer or snack, the seed-coat removal must thwart such discoveries. Besides, the fava bean can no doubt serve just as easily for any of those possibilities. I don't particularly recommend cooking your own lupini. But if you insist, don't make the same mistake I did. You absolutely must soak them for about 3 days in well-salted water with several changes of water. I tried salting the beans after cooking, but never got rid of the bitterness, which made them inedible.

Lupini Serving Suggestion

Drain a jar of lupini. Spread the beans on a bed of redleaf or romaine lettuce and sprinkle them with a fragrant olive oil, salt, pepper, and chopped fresh parsley, basil, or thyme.

Mung Beans

Chances are, you've heard more about mung sprouts than about mung beans. The sprouts are popular in Chinese cooking and are often available in supermarkets. They have pearly white flesh, are about the size of thick spaghetti, and add nice texture and mild vegetable flavor to fresh salads (blanched first) or stir-fries.

The beans themselves are a drab olive green and are rather small cylindrical shapes. They are a protein-rich staple in India and the East, served under various guises—in porridges, fried cakes, and as a flour made into Oriental pastas (mung bean thread). Supposedly they lack the gas-producing properties of most beans, being highly digestible. They may be the basis of Indian dhals (a cooked puree of pulses), too, spiced with hot and aromatic seasonings.

Mung beans must be rehydrated like other dried beans, then simmered for 1 to 1½ hours until tender. They make a good substitute for adzuki, soybeans, or lentils. They are generally sold in most natural-food stores or in Oriental food shops. They store well, but protect them from light, heat, and moisture.

Mung Bean Potato Patties

 *4 servings*

1 cup dried mung beans
4 medium-size unpeeled potatoes
½ pound carrots, peeled and sliced
1 egg
2 tablespoons peanut oil
½ teaspoon black pepper
½ teaspoon salt
¼ cup chopped fresh parsley
½ cup grated Pecorino-Romano cheese
1 cup bread crumbs
Vegetable oil for frying

1. Soak beans in 5 cups water for at least 6 hours. Drain and cover with 5 cups fresh water. Cook until tender, about 45 minutes. Drain excess water.
2. While beans are cooking, boil potatoes and carrots until tender. Drain, mash together in a large bowl, and set aside.
3. Combine beans with mashed carrots and potatoes. Mix in egg, peanut oil, pepper, salt, parsley, and cheese. Shape into patties and coat with bread crumbs.
4. Heat vegetable oil in a large skillet. Fry patties on both sides

until nicely browned. Serve on sesame seed buns or whole-grain bread with sprouts, or shredded lettuce, tomato, and dressing of choice. Or serve as an entrée with rice.

Soybeans, Tofu, and Other Soy Foods

Soybeans are hardly a new food. Having the highest quality of all vegetable protein, they sustained many cultures in various processed forms throughout ancient Asia (where livestock was rare) for millennia. Soybeans and their offspring soy foods, including tofu, sprouts, bean cakes called *tempeh*, and soymilk, have been staples for health-food enthusiasts since the early sixties in this country.

But now soybeans are worthy of note as the basis of current mainstream foods. Soybeans yield the tofu that goes into Tofutti, the nondairy ice cream that took over the dessert food scene a while back the way frozen yogurt once had. Tofutti, like frozen yogurt, has merits and demerits. It has no cholesterol or lactose, but it does contain fat and sugar, thus its share of "empty" calories. There's no need to avoid Tofutti, any more than you should totally avoid ice cream. But it is a good idea to consume it in moderation.

Of all the soy foods, **tofu** has the most promise and appeal and it truly needn't be overwhelmed with sugar, fat, and salt to taste good. Tofu is the refined essence of the soybean's own goodness, a low-saturated-fat, cholesterol-free, high-protein food. Tofu, minus the fiber of the beans, is much more digestible, plus it is low in sodium and, if solidified with calcium coagulant, contributes a worthy amount of calcium. One gram of usable tofu protein contains about 12 calories. Eggs and beef contain about three to five times that many calories per usable gram of protein—plus the fat and cholesterol.

There are no nutritional drawbacks to tofu, only cosmetic ones. Just about anybody I talk to who avoids tofu refers to its unappealing cottony, spongy presence in tubs of cloudy water. I can't say I blame anyone who is turned off by this unfortunate, but necessary way of storing tofu. But then, a lot of meat products look terribly gruesome to me in their raw state. (Perhaps pink tofu is not a bad idea.)

Tofu can only star in a dish with a strong supporting cast of other characters. It needs to be enlivened with seasonings, sauces, marinades, and other assertive ingredients. It makes a good substitute for ricotta and cottage cheese dishes, but only with careful attention to this seasoning balance, as in the Tofu-Spinach Lasagna recipe that follows.

Once you are fond enough of tofu to keep it around regularly, try this very quick and easy treatment for sandwiches: Cut a 1-pound block of tofu into slices. Place them in a shallow plastic container with an airtight top. Sprinkle about 1/4 cup soy sauce and 1/4 cup cider or wine vinegar into the container. And 1 tablespoon chopped fresh ginger and 1 clove garlic, minced. Sprinkle in a few drops of Oriental sesame oil, if desired. Cover and shake to coat all pieces of tofu. Let marinate for 1 hour, turning occasionally, or refrigerate for up to two weeks (the tofu keeps longer this way). Use the marinated slices on whole grain bread along with slices of tomato, cucumber, sprouts, or, for a nice tangy bite, with slices of pickled ginger. It's a most delicious and healthy sandwich, and makes a nice brown-bag lunch for work. You can also add it to stir-fried vegetable dishes or heat it and serve as a high-protein entrée along with rice or potatoes.

If you don't marinate the tofu, store it in a container with water, which you should change at least every other day. For the freshest flavor, use tofu within a week or sooner.

Soymilk is the creamy almond-colored liquid made from the cooked, pureed, strained beans. It is curdled to make tofu, the way dairy milk is curdled into cottage cheese. Soymilk holds interest for anyone who desires to cut down on dairy intake. Two problems prevent soymilk from becoming more popular: inferior taste and superior price. The traditionally made soymilk is beany tasting, requiring too much sweetener to mask the flavor. Natural-foods manufacturers have found the processing to make some very creamy-textured, good-tasting soy beverages, but at about 75 cents per six-ounce serving, which is several times higher than traditional soymilk.

Tempeh, a cake of cooked soybeans inoculated with a beneficial mold (much the way blue cheese or yogurt is), is one of the hardest soy foods for the West to stomach, though it does have wide appeal for many. Tempeh burgers served in vegetarian restaurants are usually very tasty and popular. The tempeh itself has a winy, mushroomlike flavor that needs slight cooking and some seasoning to bring out its best. Tempeh is even higher in protein than tofu, has more fiber, and is slightly higher in calories. You can find tempeh in health-food stores in the freezer section.

Soybeans, small tan ovals, are easily available in supermarkets or natural-foods stores. They require soaking to rehydrate them, and a long cooking—up to 2 hours. They always remain somewhat firm and can stand in for any other dried bean in soups, salads, and casseroles. However, after a long period of cooking soybeans, I've decided to absorb their goodness in the more versatile and tastier processed forms of tofu and tempeh.

Tofu-Spinach Lasagna

 *6 to 8 servings*

This is a good way to introduce the uninitiated to tofu—they'll never guess. You can use all tofu instead of the ricotta, too.

¾ pound tofu, drained
1 cup ricotta cheese
1 10-ounce package frozen spinach, thawed

2 eggs
½ cup grated Parmesan cheese
½ cup chopped fresh parsley or basil
1 teaspoon dried marjoram or oregano
2 cloves garlic, minced
½ teaspoon black pepper
3 cups marinara sauce
1½ pounds lasagna noodles, cooked
3 cups grated mozzarella

1. Mash tofu in a large mixing bowl. With a large wooden spoon, stir in ricotta, spinach, eggs, Parmesan, parsley or basil, marjoram or oregano, garlic, and pepper and mix well.

2. Preheat oven to 350°F. Spread some sauce on the bottom of a 9-x-13-inch baking dish. Line bottom of dish with a layer of noodles. Spread a thin layer of tofu mixture on top of this. Sprinkle some mozzarella over tofu, then some more sauce. Continue layering this way, finishing with a top layer of noodles, sauce, and grated cheese. You may have leftover noodles.

3. Bake for 30 to 45 minutes until nicely browned. Serve hot.

Barbecued Tempeh

 *4 servings*

1 cup tomato puree
1 tablespoon soy sauce
1 tablespoon Dijon-style mustard
2 tablespoons wine vinegar
¼ cup minced onion
2 tablespoons minced green pepper
1 tablespoon sugar
⅛ teaspoon cayenne pepper
1 pound tempeh, cut into 1-inch squares

Preheat oven to 375°F. Combine all ingredients except tempeh. Mix well. Stir tempeh pieces into barbecue sauce. Pour into a greased baking dish. Bake for 30 minutes. Serve with rice as an entrée or on rolls.

Variations: Add 2 teaspoons curry power or chili powder. Or substitute a small hot chili for the green pepper.

Winged Beans

There are those who believe that soybeans can end world hunger. In theory and on paper it makes sense. The bean is low-cost, easy to grow, nitrogen-fixing (good to the land), and translates into many high-protein, easily digestible foods.

The winged bean, for not dissimilar reasons, may very well be another future hope for the soy optimists. A tropical legume grown in New Guinea and in parts of Southeast Asia, the bean includes a noteworthy amount of vegetable protein, as well as some calcium and iron. Its pods, leaves, seeds, shoots, and tubers are all highly edible. The crop is making its way to other parts of the world, though unlike the hardy soybean plant, winged beans survive only in tropical climes. Tropical growers delight in this plant, which resists disease, produces a high yield, and grows swiftly. For obvious reasons, horticulturalists would like to get the crop to survive in more temperate climates.

The bean pods have four ridged wings down their length. Their mild flavor when cooked is like that of a lima bean or a fresh green bean. You can find winged beans in produce markets carrying exotic or specialty items. Choose small pods that are firm and succulent, not shriveled or old. Wrap in plastic, refrigerate, and use within a few days. Cook them as you would fresh green beans or Brussels sprouts—simply steamed, boiled, and buttered, or sautéed, stir-fried, in soups, stews, casseroles, or with other vegetables. Slice them French-style to make bite-size pieces. Season them strongly with fiery tomato sauces or gently with cream sauces. Marinate in sweet-and-sour sauces or dress with vinaigrettes.

Oriental-Style Winged Beans

 *4 to 6 servings*

2 tablespoons peanut oil
1 pound winged beans, cleaned and cut into 1-inch pieces
1 sweet red pepper, finely diced
¼ cup oyster sauce (available at Oriental food stores)

1. Heat oil in wok. Stir in beans and pepper. Cook on high heat, stirring constantly, for 3 to 5 minutes, just until beans are crisp-tender.

2. Stir in oyster sauce, cover, and remove from heat. Let sit for 1 minute, then serve.

NUTS AND SEEDS

Ginkgo Nut

The fruit of the mature female ginkgo tree (*Ginkgo biloba*) is called the *ginkgo nut*. The tree, a native of China, has been grown in Japan for centuries, and can now be seen lining American streets and parks. The pretty peach-colored flesh covering the nut has a repugnant odor, not indicative of the nut's flavor or aroma qualities. The malodorous flesh, once removed, reveals the enclosed nut.

When raw, the nuts are white, but they turn a pale greenish yellow during cooking. They are about the size of a Bing cherry and are important in Japanese cooking—in savory custards, and boiled, steamed, or stir-fried dishes. Skewered and grilled, or fried and added to other dishes, they contribute color and mild, sweet, crisp flavor.

Like many other nuts in the market, ginkgo nuts are available starting in the autumn. Store them in the refrigerator for several weeks. Canned ginkgo nuts have little to offer.

Macadamia Nut

Macadamia nuts seem to be all extremes: they're high in calories—200 per eight nuts—high in fat, low in protein, and high in price. They're also extremely addictive, with an irresistibly meltable buttery texture and taste. Given all the right prerequisites, macadamias have naturally gravitated to the snack tray, though some extravagant cooks have worked them into tarts, cakes, cookies, other baked goods, and ice cream.

These tan spheres, the shape of large hazelnuts, are tropical, coming from Hawaii and California. Macadamias are most often sold shelled, as their hard shell requires the power of a bodybuilder to crack. You can use macadamias as you would any other nut, provided you're prepared to pay the price in cents and fat calories. Grind them into tortes, chop them into tart, crêpe, or pie filling, pound them to a heavenly butter to use as a sauce, blended with fresh herbs, for fish or meat.

Due to their high oil content, macadamias can go rancid rather quickly at room temperature, so refrigerate or freeze them in airtight containers and use within two months.

Macadamia-Stuffed Mushrooms

 *4 servings*

½ cup macadamia nuts, lightly toasted and finely chopped
¼ cup grated Pecorino-Romano cheese
1 garlic clove, minced
¼ cup minced fresh parsley
3 tablespoons olive oil
10 to 12 large mushroom caps

Preheat oven to 400° F. Combine nuts, cheese, garlic, parsley, and oil. Spoon filling into mushroom caps and place in an oiled baking dish. Bake for 20 minutes, or until mushrooms release juices and tops are lightly golden. Serve hot.

Pignoli (Pine Nuts)

Pine nuts are the rich-tasting stash of certain pine cones. Several species of pine tree produce the edible nuts, while others' seeds have the lure of turpentine. Indians of the Southwest, where the cream-colored nut is found, have long savored its soft butteriness. It is known as *piñon* in Spain, where it is also popular, but the Italian variety, *pignoli*, is the most highly prized.

Most popular recipes featuring pine nuts today are of Mediterranean origin. The Genovese basil sauce pesto (see recipe that follows) is probably the best-known use for pine nuts. Traditionally the nuts are pounded in a mortar and pestle along with garlic, fresh basil, olive oil, and Parmesan cheese. Greek dolmas, or stuffed grape leaves, incorporate pine nuts, and Middle Easterners add them along with other nuts and dried fruit to savory grain pilafs. A popular Italian cookie with almond flavoring also uses pine nuts. They are very expensive, but are needed only in small amounts to impart their special pine-scented sweetness.

The elongated or roundish nuts are usually ¼ to 2 inches long. They are high in oil, and their sweet piny flavor is very volatile. Store them in the refrigerator and use within two months.

Pesto Sauce

Makes 2 cups

enough for 2 to 2½ pounds of pasta

I varied this classic sauce by toasting the nuts first for richer pine-nut flavor and aroma.

1 large clove garlic
2½ cups packed basil leaves
½ cup pine nuts, lightly toasted
1 cup fragrant virgin olive oil
¾ cups grated Parmesan or Pecorino-Romano cheese

1. *By hand:* Pound the garlic, basil, and nuts in a mortar and pestle. Stir in oil and cheese.
2. *By food processor:* Place garlic, basil, and nuts in work bowl of processor, fitted with metal blade. Pulse until mixture is coarsely chopped. Then, with motor on, pour oil through feed tube. Process until sauce is smooth. Pour into bowl or container and stir in cheese.

Spoon over cooked pasta, baked potatoes, or tomatoes, or add to salad dressings. Store sauce in refrigerator for up to 2 weeks.

HERBS and SPICES

Herbs and spices are often the very definition of one cuisine or another—the curry of India, the basil and oregano of Mediterranean cooking, the ginger and Szechuan pepper of Chinese cooking, to name a few examples. Opening our taste buds to a new spectrum of flavors helps get us away from the ubiquitous salt and pepper shakers. What a worthwhile contribution to the pleasure and health aspects of our diet!

Try to get herbs and spices as fresh as possible and from a reputable dealer. Buy dried herbs and spices in small amounts and store for the shortest time possible—always away from light, heat, and moisture. Nothing beats fresh herbs, which demand has made more and more available in produce markets. Store them as you would fresh greens (see page 54).

Capers

Capers are immature flower buds that grow wild in the Mediterranean climate on a short shrub, *Capparis spinosa*, which reaches all of 3 feet. The green buckshotlike buds go into condiments as mundane as tartar sauce and a dish as elegant as veal piccata. The aromatic seeds also appear in rémoulade and ravigote sauces, and a tomato-sweet eggplant appetizer called *caponata* (see recipe that follows), also available canned from the manufacturer Progresso.

The little seeds are pickled in a vinegar and salt brine, but have much more panache than a mere gherkin. Like green olives, capers develop their unique flavor in the brine marinade. They are small, but they explode with a burst of lemony tang that works well in smooth sauces of butter or cream, especially on fish, chicken, or veal.

Their expense owes to the slowness in collecting the buds from the bush, but they are potent and needed only in small amounts. Always keep the capers covered in their brine. Capers may be added to sauces drained or along with their sharp marinade, depending on how much piquancy is required. The pickled buds keep for a good long time in the refrigerator.

Caponata

 *Makes about 1½ quarts*

½ cup olive oil
1 large onion, chopped
3 small eggplants (about 2½ pounds), cubed
2 ribs celery, minced
1 small green pepper, minced
2 pounds Italian plum tomatoes, chopped
½ cup pitted Italian olives, sliced
½ cup red wine
1½ tablespoons sugar
¼ cup capers, drained
½ teaspoon black pepper
2 tablespoons red wine vinegar

1. Heat oil in a large pot. Toss in onion and eggplant and stir over moderately high heat for about 5 minutes. Stir in celery and green pepper and cook another 5 minutes, until eggplant is almost tender.

2. Stir in tomatoes and olives, bring to a boil, then lower to a simmer and cook for 30 minutes. Add wine, sugar, capers, and black pepper and cook another 15 minutes. Stir in vinegar and turn into a heatproof serving dish. Allow to reach room temperature before serving. Serve as an appetizer with bread, crackers, cheese, or celery and carrot sticks, or as a condiment on sandwiches. It's great on open-face grilled cheese. Refrigerate for up to 2 weeks. May also be canned.

Cardamom

East Indian dishes, a Swedish yellow cake, and the rich syrupy Turkish coffee of a favorite neighborhood Middle Eastern restaurant—these were the ways I was introduced to the Oriental spice cardamom. The once little-known spice gets around, and it is most definitely a good one—as useful as cinnamon—to keep on hand. Its warmly pungent taste and fragrance tickle my nostrils the way frankincense in church ceremonies once did.

The cardamom plant, a ginger relative, is indigenous to Ceylon, growing wild with beautiful mauve-veined leaves in wet forests. The fully ripe cardamom fruit is deep yellow. The whole seed is a creamy white, brown, or almond three-sided ovoid capsule with longitudinal wrinkles. The outer shell, or pericarp, is papery and tough and must be removed to release the aromatic seed within. The inner seed is the part rife with aroma and ginger-lemon spiciness. Cardamom is sold whole, decorticated (its fibrous hull removed), or ground.

The heady-scented spice often contributes to the sweeter side of a complex curry blend. It also scents and flavors breads, pastries, cakes, cookies, sausage, and other seasoning blends. To obtain the full range of cardamom's floral depth, you must hull the seeds as needed. Do so easily with a mortar and pestle or spice grinder, then sift the seed from the hull. Some dishes use the seed whole— the way cinnamon stick may be used—and remove it after cooking. The seed may also be roasted to heighten its warming sweetness. The powdered cardamom is not nearly so potent as the freshly ground, but I've found it to have some worth if used within a few months. Buy the powdered spice in small amounts.

Chervil

Chervil is an herb of delicate nuance, with shades of its close kin parsley and of licorice-flavored tarragon. Its standard roles are time-honored, but it is another "born-again" ingredient, earning recognition anew as cooks opt for the fresh and the homegrown. Chervil is an element in the classic *fines herbes* mixture. Its herbal quality, more fleeting than that of parsley, has often been paired with omelets, poultry, veal, and béarnaise sauce.

Today, avant-garde chefs have endowed the herb with new and successful roles: atop shellfish, salmon, fresh greens, and in vinaigrettes, in herb-flavored butters and potato-leek soup.

Chervil was an ancient herbal elixir during the Middle Ages. Monks grew it in their monastery "medicine gardens," recognizing the herb's diuretic and purgative quality. In addition, Pliny the Elder, the Roman herbalist, recommended chervil "to comfort the cold stomach of the aged." And its boiled roots were supposed to ward off the plague.

But never boil this gentle herb today or you'll ward off its delicate taste. Always add it near the end of cooking, so the heat just disperses its flavor. The fresh has so much more character than the soulless dried that if you can't find fresh leafy chervil (summer's its peak season), buy a packet of seeds and grow your own.

Salmon-Potato Salad with Chervil

 *2 to 4 servings*

1½ pounds salmon fillets, poached and chunked
6 small red potatoes, cooked and quartered
¼ cup minced scallions
¼ cup seeded and chopped cucumber
2 tablespoons white wine vinegar
1 teaspoon sugar
¼ teaspoon salt
1 hard-cooked egg, finely chopped
¾ cup mayonnaise
¼ cup chopped fresh chervil
Lettuce leaves

Combine salmon, potatoes, scallions, and cucumbers. Combine remaining ingredients except for lettuce. Toss dressing with salad. Chill for 1 hour and serve on a bed of lettuce.

Coriander (Cilantro)

The same ancient spice that scented Egyptian tombs and the Hanging Gardens of Babylon is today a necessary flavoring agent in the ever-pedestrian hot dog. Coriander leaves and seeds have had loftier niches in Mexican, Chinese, and Indian cuisines.

Botanically *coriander* refers to the whole plant, which is a member of the parsley family. In cook's jargon, *coriander* most often refers to the plant's small round white to yellowish brown seeds. *Cilantro* generally indicates the plant's foliage, which very much resembles Italian flat-leaf parsley, but with shorter stems and fan-shaped, crinkle-edged leaves. Cilantro is also known as *Chinese* or *Mexican parsley*.

THE LEAVES

The authors of the *Joy of Cooking* (New American Library, 1985) refer to the cilantro leaves' fetid odor and taste, but I am inclined to side with those who prize the herb's more justly "fragrant" character. I know at least two simple dishes—Chinese crisp whole fish and a Mexican burrito—made infinitely more complex by a flourish of crushed fresh cilantro leaves.

Cilantro's pungency unfolds best when it is used as a garnish. Try a modest sprinkling of chopped cilantro on hot buttered carrots. The fresh leaves are the correct ingredient to use in many Mexican salsas, but try this lively garnish on almost any tomato-based dish—gazpacho, chili, a simple tomato soup or salad. Cilantro is a natural foil for Chinese-style barbecued beef, smoked duck with plum sauce, and many pork and fish dishes. Add a refreshingly different taste to any cheese-, meat-, or vegetable-based omelet with a few pinches of minced cilantro.

When buying fresh cilantro (ignore the dried version, which has lost too much flavor), or any fresh herb, look for crisp, not limp or wilted, leaves sporting bright color. The fresh leaves won't keep well for more than three to four days. Refrigerate them, wrapped in a paper towel. The leaves will lose some seasoning power, but you can chop and freeze them without blanching.

THE SEEDS

Unlike the leaves, coriander seeds—available whole or ground—impart a more mild and delicate fragrance to foods. Somewhat orangy and citruslike, this flavor has for decades provided the spice and scent so welcome in baked goods such as gingerbread and apple pie. The whole seeds have appeared in old-fashioned candies called "comfits," in sausages, and as a component of pickling spices. No curry is worth its spunk without coriander.

Coriander seeds, which are imported from Morocco, Romania, or Argentina, are about ⅛ inch in diameter and striped with alternating straight and wavy ridges. Most every grocer's rack stocks this spice. Some Indian recipes call for grinding the whole seeds; it is best to dry-roast the seeds in a heavy skillet just until crisp—to enhance flavor and ensure a finer grind.

Store coriander as you would other spices, away from moisture and heat. Garam Masala (page 201), a popular curry blend that you can add to any vegetable, meat, or fish combination, any soup or stir-fry, is made with coriander. Its flavor develops best when allowed at least 10 minutes to cook.

Cumin

In North African open-air markets, small mountains of ground cumin send an overpowering acrid aroma into the air. The emphatic spice, with its distinct earthiness, pervades the cuisine of that region. A native of Egypt and the Mediterranean, cumin is also grown in Iran, Morocco, Turkey, Sicily, and India. Used in curries and chili blends, it is very popular in Indian and Mexican cooking, but not particularly in European cooking. Cumin comes as whole long brownish seeds resembling caraway, to which it is related, or ground as a powder.

Cumin seed or powder is often toasted in a heavy skillet to round out its almost mentholated flavor before it is added to a dish or spice blend. There is no mistaking cumin, for it has a distinguishable strong aroma and taste that is not for timid palates and can be overdone. In their rather dated book *Garden Spice and Wild Pot-Herbs*, published in 1955, when Americans were steeped in a decade of little imagination, authors Walter Muenscher and Myron Arthur Rice note that "cumin seed, because of its peculiar flavor, is used only in veterinary medicine."

Happily, other cultures remained naïve as to this staid advice. In the right balance cumin is a very good spice. Falafel, Middle Eastern fried chick-pea patties, would seem off without their dose of cumin. The Romans, our most original culinary trendsetters, once substituted cumin's vibrant pepperiness for real peppers when the latter were hard to come by. Cumin seeds are also popular in cheeses, breads, sausages, and with vegetables. The best advice regarding this richly flavored spice is to add it to food with restraint, letting its flavor develop before you decide more is needed. The ground spice keeps its perfume fairly well, but buy it in small amounts and store it away from heat and moisture.

Garam Masala

 *Makes about ¹/₂ cup*

There are as many recipes for this exotic blend as there are cooks in India. Use this pungent spice to season sauces, soups, dhals, rice-and-bean dishes, vegetables, meat, poultry, or seafood dishes.

2 3-inch sticks of cinnamon
2 tablespoons cardamom pods
1 tablespoon cumin seeds

2 teaspoons coriander seeds
2 teaspoons peppercorns
1 teaspoon whole cloves
1/2 teaspoon mace powder

1. Preheat oven to 250°F. Spread out all spices except mace on a baking sheet. Roast for 10 to 15 minutes, until spices are very fragrant, but not browning. Stir every 2 to 3 minutes to keep from browning.

2. Remove seeds from cardamom pods. Discard pods. Place all spices except mace in spice or coffee grinder or electric blender and grind to a fine powder. Mix in mace and store in an airtight jar.

Fenugreek

The color of the Grand Canyon, fenugreek seeds resemble little chips of baked Indian clay. They have a sharp, sweet smell reminiscent of celery and caramelized sugar. If you are ardently interested in Indian food, you should know fenugreek. It is a main ingredient in curries, also used in chutneys, other Indian dishes, and in North African cooking. Native to Mediterranean Europe and Asia, fenugreek is grown also in North Africa. Indians consider the leaves of the plant a delicacy that goes well with potatoes.

The seeds have had medicinal as well as culinary importance. I knew an herbal doctor in San Francisco who recommended a cleansing, calming tea made from fenugreek, fennel, and licorice, and other herbs. When soaked in water, fenugreek emits an emollient mucilage—we might call it fiber today—that soothes the intestinal tract. Fenugreek has been used in mustard plasters to soothe inflammation. The seeds are also the basis for artificial maple flavoring.

The seeds can be roasted to lessen bitterness before being ground into a spice blend. You can find fenugreek seeds wherever a good array of herbs and spices is sold, and most certainly in an Indian food store.

Curry Powder

 *Makes 2 tablespoons*

1 teaspoon cinnamon
1 teaspoon ground fenugreek (see Note)
½ teaspoon turmeric
½ teaspoon ground cardamom
½ teaspoon ground coriander
¼ teaspoon ground cloves
1½ teaspoons ground cumin
½ teaspoon dry mustard
¼ teaspoon ground ginger

Mix all spices together and store in an airtight jar.

Note: If you cannot find ground fenugreek, grind the whole seeds in a spice or coffee grinder or with a mortar and pestle.

Filé Powder

Filé powder, looking brown and dusty, is ground from the dried leaves of the sassafras plant. It is used as a thickening and flavoring agent for the popular Creole gumbo. The mucilaginous quality of the filé powder, along with that of okra, also an indispensable gumbo ingredient, gives the dish its characteristic texture. Filé powder also adds a peppery spice taste, which can be used in other condiments too. Never boil the gumbo after adding filé or a stringy texture will result. Buy filé powder in any herb and spice corner. Store it away from heat, light, and moisture.

Juniper Berries

A member of the pine clan, juniper berries (*Juniperus communis*) grow on small evergreen shrublike trees that are often cultivated as ornamentals. The blue- or gray-green leaves surround the dark-blue berry fruit. The entire shrub is aromatic, with the berries concentrating the fragrance into a bittersweetness that has medicinal and culinary uses. The berries were formerly prized for their fragrance and used to freshen stuffy rooms.

Juniper berries are enjoying rediscovery with the growing attraction to game meat. The berries have typically seasoned bean-based and game dishes, their strong flavor neutralizing the gaminess of venison and other wild animals. The meat can be marinated or braised in a stock with the berries. Steeped in liquid, the hard blue-black berries exude the flavoring that is distilled into gin spirits. They may also be added to pickling brines for meat, poultry, and sauerkraut.

The berries have their share of herbal properties too, including appetite and disgestive aid and diuretic action. In addition, juniper has been attributed with the power to ward off evil spirits.

Rabbit Stew

4 servings

1 4-pound rabbit
4 cups chicken or beef stock
3 tablespoons juniper berries
¼ pound smoked slab bacon, diced
1 large onion, chopped
6 small red potatoes
2 ribs celery, diced
4 carrots, each quartered
2 cups stewed tomatoes
1 teaspoon thyme
4 whole cloves

1. Combine rabbit, stock, and berries in a large pot and simmer for 2 hours. Drain and reserve 1 cup stock. When cooled, cut rabbit into parts.

2. Cook bacon in a large pot for 10 minutes. Add onion, potatoes, celery, and carrots. Cover and cook 15 minutes, stirring occasionally.

3. Stir in tomatoes, thyme, cloves, and reserved stock. Simmer, uncovered, for 30 minutes. Add rabbit and simmer about 20 minutes longer. Serve hot.

Lemongrass

Lemongrass has been some of the best culinary news in the past few years. It is pungent and flowery, with a most complex fresh lemony bouquet. This tropical herb (*Cymbopogon citratus*) is used very often in the cooking of Southeast Asia, its citrus notes a welcome foil for the piquancy of many Thai soups. Also called *sereh*, or *serei*, lemongrass resembles long reeds of matte-green grass with a slightly bulbous base like that of a scallion. It contains the same active ingredient in lemon peel, citral.

Its perfumed potency is welcomed by most American cooks and diners who try it. Lemongrass is commonly infused through soups, stews, sauces, along with the most highly aromatic ingredients— ginger, chilies, cilantro, garlic. It is available fresh in many Oriental markets and dried in health-food stores to be made into beverage tea. As a seasoning herb, the fresh is preferable. Its fresh fragrance can be diffused through cooking or the herb can be used raw as a garnish. Though the dried herb makes a relaxing infusion, this version possesses only a wisp of its former seasoning power.

You can refrigerate fresh lemongrass for up to ten days or freeze it indefinitely and use as needed, slicing off slivers. Since fresh lemongrass is powerful, and develops with cooking, use it sparingly until you understand its potency. Add slivers (which are mostly fibrous and inedible and must be removed before serving) to soups, stews, fish poaching liquids, and rice dishes, or make a relaxing beverage by steeping leaves in boiled water.

Snapper with Spicy Lemongrass Cream

 *4 servings*

Use the sauce in this recipe for any type of fish or shellfish, including broiled or poached shrimp, crab, or lobster.

4 snapper fillets (about 1½ pounds)
3 cups fish stock
2 tablespoons chopped fresh lemongrass

1 clove garlic, mashed
3 quarter-size slices fresh ginger
1 cup heavy cream
2 tablespoons butter
2 tablespoons chopped fresh herb—parsley, cilantro, chervil, tarragon (optional)

1. Place fillets in a lightly greased baking dish with a cover (or cover a pan with foil). Bake at 350°F. for about 20 minutes, until fish is flaky and loses its translucency.

2. Prepare sauce while fish cooks: Combine stock, lemongrass, garlic, and ginger in a heavy saucepan and boil uncovered until reduced to about 1 cup.

3. Stir in cream and simmer until reduced to 1½ cups sauce. Strain through a sieve or cheesecloth and return to saucepan.

4. Place cooked fish on a serving platter. Stir butter into cream sauce and heat just until butter is melted. Pour sauce over fish, garnish with herb, and serve immediately.

Mace

Mace, the rust-colored powder that is a silent partner in pumpkin pie spice (see recipe below) and an outspoken component of Indian curries, comes from the same evergreen tree as nutmeg, native to the Moluccas, or Spice Islands. This explains why the two have similar tastes, though nutmeg is the better known of the two. Nutmeg is the seed and mace is the aril, or hull-like covering. The difference between the two is subtle but perceptible. Nutmeg is nuttier, and mace more warming, like cardamom. Mace is sold whole or ground. It is very tough and hard to grind, so buy the ground. It can be used in any way nutmeg is—in cakes, sauces, stuffings, rice and grain dishes, pickles, fruits, preserves for sweet or savory dishes. It may also be added to Indian spice blends.

Pumpkin Pie Spice

 *Makes ¼ cup*

1½ teaspoons mace
½ teaspoon ground cloves
4 teaspoons ground nutmeg
4 teaspoons ground cinnamon
2 teaspoons ground ginger

Combine all spices and mix well. Store in an airtight jar.

Saffron

A few crimson-gold threads of saffron are all it takes to color paella, bouillabaisse, risottos, or Indian rice mixtures. Cakes and breads can also be laced with these flighty wisps, which are worth their weight in gold. The tubular florets of orange-red are the dried stigmas of a flower. It takes sixty thousand stigmas of saffron to make a pound. The precious spice is mostly indispensable to those bent on authenticity and is more prized for its luscious sunny color than for its pungent taste.

Saffron once grew wild in Greece and Asia Minor, but now must be cultivated. The precious brilliant spice was used as a perfume and as a dye until this became too extravagant. Aromatic and sharp tasting, too much saffron overpowers and borders on an unpleasant medicinal flavor. Only a smidgeon is required to color and flavor a dish. The threads may be gently roasted, then crumbled into a liquid to release their flavor and color properties.

If you don't see saffron with the other spices, ask for it. Its outrageous price seems to justify petty larceny for some, so shopkeepers often shelve it in a shoplift-proof spot. A bargain price probably indicates that the spice has been stretched with cheaper adulterants such as arnica, calendula petals, or safflower florets.

Saffron Rice with Peas and Red Pepper

 *4 servings*

1 teaspoon saffron
4 cups boiling water
2 cups long-grain rice
1 10-ounce package frozen peas
½ teaspoon salt
1 small red pepper, minced

Toast saffron in a heavy-bottomed saucepan, a couple of minutes, just until fragrant. Pour in water and bring to a boil. Add remaining ingredients, lower heat, cover, and simmer until water is absorbed, about 20 minutes. Serve hot.

Star Anise

Star anise, like Szechuan peppers, is an Asian ingredient, likely to become a standard as chefs become more eclectic, giving it play in and out of Asian-style cooking. This ancient spice of the Levant is licorice flavored like Western anise, but more strongly so and slightly more bitter. Star anise, belonging to the magnolia family, is not related to the anise we grow here. It is a brown pod, star-shaped, with six or eight points. It is used whole as a garnish, broken up, or crushed to intensify the flavor it gives to meat or poultry. It adds a nice surprise to sauces. It is one of the Chinese Five Spices, also called Five-Spice Powder or five-fragrance powder (see recipe following), along with cassia or cinnamon, cloves, fennel seed, and pepper or ginger. Star anise is imported from China and is expensive.

Chinese Five-Spice Powder

 *Makes about ¹/₃ cup*

1 3-inch cinnamon stick
4 whole star anise
3 teaspoons whole cloves
3 teaspoons fennel seeds
2 teaspoons peppercorns

Grind all spices in a spice or coffee grinder to a fine powder. Store in an airtight container. Use in marinades, stir-fries, or rub into meat or poultry before roasting.

Szechuan Peppers

These aromatic rusty-brown peppercorns, also called *fagara* and *Chinese* or *wild pepper*, are not piping hot, but spicy, mildly piquant, and fragrant. They are not even related to the black peppercorns they resemble. They are the dried berry of the shrub *Zanthoxylum piperitum*, a tree in the citrus family, which grows in any temperate climate. The Chinese often mix this peppery spice with salt, sometimes roasting it first. The chefs who are helping to forge a new American cuisine have taken to rubbing the berries into roasted meats and poultry, to which they lend new taste dimensions. The best way to release their woodsy flavor fully is with a few minutes toasting in a heavy skillet. The berries are then crushed to a coarse powder in a mortar and pestle or with a spice grinder. They can also be steeped whole or crushed in marinades for meat or fish. Or you can place them in a peppermill and grind fresh over food as you would black pepper. They are available in specialty shops and Chinese groceries in plastic packages. Store them in an airtight container.

Szechuan Roasted Chicken

 *4 servings*

1 clove garlic, pressed
2 teaspoons minced fresh ginger
²/₃ cup dry sherry
¹/₃ cup soy sauce
¹/₄ cup peanut oil
1 teaspoon Chinese Five-Spice Powder (see page 210)

1 4-pound chicken
2 teaspoons Szechuan peppers

1. Combine garlic, ginger, sherry, soy sauce, oil, and Five-Spice Powder in a deep bowl and mix well. Place chicken in bowl and spoon marinade over it to coat well. Marinate at least 2 hours, turning several times.
2. Toast the peppercorns in a frying pan over moderate heat, shaking the pan, until they start to smoke, 3 to 5 minutes. Grind to a coarse powder in a mortar and pestle or electric spice grinder.
3. Preheat oven to 400°F. Sprinkle pepper all over chicken. Place chicken on a rack, skin side up, in a shallow roasting pan and roast for 3 minutes. Turn heat down to 350° and cook until juices run clear when leg is pierced, about 30 minutes. Remove from oven and allow to set 10 minutes before serving.

Turmeric

Turmeric powder, ground from a yellow rhizome (*Curcuma longa*) native to Malabar in India, is one of those low-key but crucial spices that is given more shelf space now that spicy food is on the upswing. On its own it gives mellow warmth and scarlet-orange color to dishes, but it is almost always a component of a larger spice blend. Turmeric's taste, musky and slightly bitter, is an important ingredient in curries. It is on the mild end of the spectrum, primarily lending its fiery color to the mixture, but must be used in small quantities or it will make the curry bitter. Though related to ginger and cardamom, it is not nearly as aromatic as those two.

The bright spice has preservative properties and is also added to pickles and mustards. Some cooks use its sunrise brilliance to replace saffron. It is sometimes dissolved in alcohol to yield a food coloring. Turmeric is a great team player, but rarely the lead seasoning used for its own merit, unless just its shading is desired. Some of the spices that support it well are cumin, dried mustard, ground coriander and cardamom, ginger, and garlic. Chicken and fish dishes, cream sauces, eggs, relish, rice and grain dishes, and soups, especially creamed ones, perk up with a jot of turmeric in conjunction with any of these spices. (See Curry Powder recipe, page 203.)

SPECIALTY

VINEGARS and OILS

Our taste for new foods has been refined in part by our greater appreciation for a broad array of vinegars and cooking oils and their subtle powers of seasoning.

VINEGARS

Like salt, vinegar is one of the oldest condiments used to season, preserve, and tenderize food. Vinegar has made an indelible mark on the cooking of just about every culture. Discerning cooks today tap such time-honored uses as one more new source of inspiration. Its tangy traits appear in marinades, pickles, dressings, relishes, and many a condiment. All vinegars, which are actually intentionally soured wines, have a preservative quality, owing to their 4 percent to 7 percent acidity. Like wine, too, vinegar can be shades of mellow, sharp, sour, and sweet. Vinegars owe their specific characteristics largely to their source and sometimes to fermentation techniques. There are no hard-and-fast rules for vinegar. Just be sure it amplifies, doesn't overpower, any food you dress with it. Here are some general guidelines for different types of vinegars.

Balsamic vinegar Produced in Modena, Italy, has a 6 percent acidity and is one of the most flavorful vinegars. It is as dark as soy sauce and lustily sweet and woodsy, perhaps owing to its long aging period. It is a great enhancer of fresh pungent garden greens, boiled or steamed vegetables, roasted meats, and poached fish. Use it alone as a seasoning if you like, but with restraint as it overpowers easily. Olive oil is its natural ally. It goes well with nut oils, too.

Champagne wine vinegar Has a 6 percent to 7 percent acidity. It may be distilled in France from champagne or chardonnay wine. Slightly fruitier than white wine vinegar, it is used to dress salads or to add vim and vigor to sauces. It is expensive.

Cider vinegar Fermented from apple juice, has about 5 percent to 6 percent acetic acid and a pronounced apple-acid flavor. It is a good marinade vinegar for vegetables and condiments. It works well in salad dressings, too, especially with strong or aromatic ingredients, such as soy sauce, dill, or tomatoes. Peanut or sesame oils are a good match for cider vinegar.

Malt vinegar Made from barley malt or other cereal grains, is essentially a beer vinegar. Though not as sour as wine vinegars, it is flatter, with much less range of flavor and a 5 percent to 6 percent acidity. Some cooks prefer to use it mainly for its preservative quality, but not much as a taste enhancer, while others use it as they would any vinegar.

Rice vinegar Distilled from rice, has less sharpness than cider vinegar and a hint of sweetness. The Japanese use rice vinegar to make sushi, dipping sauces, and many pickled dishes. I find it is good in marinating tofu along with soy sauce and ginger, and also good in grain and bean salads.

Sherry wine vinegar Is distilled from sherry, the best, of course, coming from Spain, where this spirit originates, and aged in oak casks. It has about 6 percent acidity, is robust and malty and very expensive. Its most common use is as the tart ingredient in sauces. Its caramel richness may also be used to baste meats, or to splash into finished soups or stews.

White or distilled vinegar   Distilled from alcohol, is strong, acidic, and generally too sharp for dressings and regular cooking. It may be used in canning for its preservative quality.

Wine vinegars   With about 5 percent acetic acid content, may derive from red, white, or rosé wines. They are robust and perceptibly fruity and go well with green salads and in most sauces and dressings. Red wine vinegar, of course, has its standard role in Italian dressings. White wine vinegar is slightly more delicate and is often infused with an herb or spice, or used as the basis for fruit vinegars.

FLAVORED VINEGARS

In addition to different degrees of sourness or tartness, acidity, and other traits a vinegar's essence can be tinged with the sweetness of fruits, the tang of an herb, the fragrance of a spice, or a blend of all three. The flavorful results transcend the mere addition of tartness to food. Steeping herbs and spices in vinegars suspends their floral essence for use in marinades and salad dressings. Make your own aromatic infusion by choosing a single herb—basil, tarragon, rosemary, for example—or a mixed bouquet, adding garlic, peppercorns, cinnamon sticks, ginger, coriander seeds, or any spice blend. Place the vinegar, herbs (preferably fresh), and spices in clear wine bottles with clamp-type porcelain caps or tight-fitting corks.

Berry and fruit vinegars have enjoyed a popularity that continues to give them shelf space in specialty-food stores. Sprinkle their fruity sweetness over fruit or vegetable salads, poultry, or fish. I've used the following raspberry vinegar on potato salads, over steamed greens, and in creamy vinaigrettes.

Raspberry Vinegar

 *Makes 2 cups*

2 cups white wine vinegar
2 tablespoons sugar
1 cup raspberries (you may substitute any other berries)

1. Combine vinegar and sugar and heat almost to boiling, just until sugar is dissolved.
2. Place berries and vinegar in a jar with a tight-fitting non-corrosive lid. Cool before sealing over tightly. Allow to steep several days before using. Store for up to six months

Note: All vinegars are corrosive. Therefore, use only glass, enamel, or stainless-steel vessels when working with vinegared foods—never aluminum or copper.

OILS

Before the current awakening to new food tastes, oil was a bland pale liquid, adding nothing more than lubrication and calories to cooking. Now inventive cooks are exploring the taste, tint, and bouquet that specialty oils can lend a dish, learning new rules for whether or not to cook an oil.

By *specialty oil* I mean those that have undergone minimal processing and refinement, so as to preserve the native flavor, aroma, and often color of the original nut, seed, or fruit source. Some heady examples include a golden-topaz fruity olive oil, a honey-tinted and toasty-scented hazelnut oil, or a buttery rich walnut oil. Different from the transparent, tasteless supermarket product, they have character. They have not been treated to high-heat pressing, chemical solvents, alkali solutions, bleaching agents, and deodorizing that neutralizes all their idiosyncrasies.

These more expensive specialty oils retain their esters and ele-

The Cook's Guide to Oils

OIL	FLAVOR	SUGGESTED USES	COMMENTS	APPROXIMATE SMOKING POINT
Almond	mildly sweet and nutty; very light, if refined	dressings for greens, vegetables; not good for cooking	contains about 70% monounsaturated fats, one of the lowest in saturated fats (8%)	—
Avocado	sweet walnutlike flavor	vinaigrette salad dressing, or mix with fresh lemon juice for bitter greens, such as arugula, chicory, watercress; not good for cooking	keeps a strong flavor even when refined; 62% monounsaturated fats	—
Corn	light, bland	deep and shallow frying; mix with strong-flavored oils in dressing; popping corn, basting	most versatile oil for all-purpose uses; 59% unsaturated fats	465°F.
Hazelnut	buttery	dressings for salads, raw vegetables	very high in monounsaturated fats (78%)	—
Olive	light to fruity to peppery (green olive oil)	frying breaded vegetables; pasta sauces, salad dressings, mayonnaise; sprinkled over Italian soups, baked chicken, or baked fish casseroles	if you buy gallon tins, decant olive oil into smaller dark glass bottles; 74% monounsaturated fats	375°F.

Oil	Flavor	Uses	Fat Composition	Smoke Point
Peanut	distinctly nutty	deep or shallow frying; dressings for raw vegetables; in potato salads	46% monounsaturated fats; 32% polyunsaturated fats	440°F.
Safflower	bland	deep and shallow frying; greasing baking tins; popping corn; to cut strong-flavored oils in cold dressings	very rich in linoleic acid (usually 70%); a polyunsaturated fat	510°F.
Sesame Seed	toasty, earthy, robust flavor	as a seasoning for cooked dishes, especially Chinese stir-fry; in marinades; along with other mild oil in salad dressing; not good for frying	only the "burnt-toast"-colored Oriental sesame oil has the unmistakable distinct flavor; clear, refined sesame is very light tasting; 42% polyunsaturated fats	420°F.
Soy	sweet beany flavor	deep and shallow frying, greasing tins, popping corn	the dark cold-pressed soy oil is much beanier and tends to foam when used in frying (it also contains more lecithin); 58% polyunsaturated fats	495°F.
Sunflower	mild hint of raw sunflower seeds	baked goods, shallow frying, mild salad dressings	percentage of polyunsaturated fats may range from 40% to 65%	480°F.
Walnut	butternut flavor	dressings with fruit-flavored vinegars for mixed greens, raw or steamed vegetables; not good for cooking	imported has a strong flavor, clear refined is more bland; 63% polyunsaturated fats	—

ments, yielding a full range of charm that is more volatile and given to quicker oxidation (causing rancidity). Here are some guidelines for storing and cooking with these specialty oils:

- Buy them in small amounts, since they turn rancid quickly. Store them away from heat and light, ideally in the refrigerator, unless advised not to (as with some olive oils). Clouding is natural under cold storage and will dissipate at room temperature.
- Minimize heating, which diminishes flavor and aroma of these oils. You'll notice dark sesame oil is generally added after a dish is cooked. Olive and avocado oils are exceptions, retaining some fruitiness with cooking.
- The best use for these highly flavored oils is in uncooked preparations, as in a light splash on peppery greens, lacing of a marinade, flavoring a vinaigrette. Almond, hazelnut, or walnut oil dressings are the robust seasoning equivalent of the new salad bowl greens such as arugula, watercress, radicchio, and chicories. Avocado oil goes well with delicate lettuce and mild-flavored vegetables.
- Mix these nut and seed oils for different flavor effects. Or cut the strength of their nutty and fruity notes with milder oils.
- If you do cook with any of these oils, note that they will burn and smoke at much lower temperatures than the refined filtered clear oils.
- From a health standpoint, all vegetable oils, except palm and coconut, are a better alternative to butter and hydrogenated fats. They never contain cholesterol. Most vegetable oils have a high ratio of polyunsaturated fatty acids, which in moderation help lower cholesterol count. Almond, avocado, hazelnut, and olive oils are higher in monounsaturated oils, which studies show may lower cholesterol levels even more effectively. However, in excess, even these "good fats" can add to heart disease risks.

The chart on the preceding pages is a handy at-a-glance guide for cooking with the various nut, seed, and fruit oils.

FLAVORS *from the*

EAST

Following are some of the key items necessary in various types of Asian cuisine.

Fermented and *Salted Black Beans*

Fermented or salted black beans are made from a variety of soybean that is black, not from the dried black or turtle bean used to make many Latin American dishes. Like other soyfoods, black beans were discovered ages ago, when Easterners learned to process soy into foods and condiments more biologically assimilable and tastier than the bean itself. These beans, like aged soy sauces, are rich, pungent, beefy, and needed in only small amounts to season dishes. They are often used with chicken, seafood, meats, and vegetables. They may be chopped or mashed, and sautéed, or they may be pureed with other ingredients to make a savory sauce. Black beans are available canned or in plastic packages in some supermarkets and in Asian food stores. They may be labeled Fermented Black Beans or Salted Black Beans. To reduce their pungency and saltiness, the beans are sometimes rinsed before using. Refrigerate them after opening.

Scallops and Shrimp with Black Bean Sauce

 *4 servings*

¼ cup oil
1½ tablespoons fermented black beans, rinsed
2 small red peppers, chopped
1 pound sea scallops
½ pound medium-sized shrimp, cleaned and deveined
2 cloves garlic, minced
1 tablespoon minced ginger
½ cup sherry
½ cup fish or chicken stock
2 teaspoons kudzu (see page 224) or cornstarch
2 tablespoons chopped fresh cilantro

1. Add 2 tablespoons of oil to a heated wok. Stir-fry beans and peppers for 2 minutes. Remove from pan.
2. Add remaining oil to wok. Stir-fry scallops and shrimp for 2 minutes. Add garlic, ginger, and black beans, and stir-fry another few minutes, until shellfish is cooked through, about 5 minutes.
3. Combine sherry, stock, and kudzu or cornstarch and stir into wok, mixing gently until sauce is thickened, about 2 minutes. Garnish with cilantro and serve immediately, accompanied with rice.

Hoisin

Hoisin is yet another soybean-based sauce, thick and chocolaty-looking, but sweetly pungent and mildly hot. Hoisin often seasons Peking duck or meat, poultry, vegetable, or seafood stir-fries. The sauce can be simply tossed with cooked food to season it. Or it can be added near the end of cooking and tossed in with the ingredients to coat them and allowed a quick high heating to diffuse its complex flavor. The thick hoisin clings to the food and adds an appealing glistening brown glaze. Refrigerate opened hoisin sauce and use within three months.

Cashew Chicken with Hoisin

 *4 servings*

2 tablespoons peanut oil
1½ pounds skinned boneless chicken breasts, cubed
½ cup hoisin sauce
3 scallions, thinly sliced
1 cup toasted cashews

Add oil to a heated wok and stir-fry chicken for 3 minutes. Stir in hoisin sauce and stir-fry another 2 minutes. Add scallions and stir-fry another minute. Toss in cashews and serve immediately.

Kudzu

While cooks in the West have mainly relied upon cornstarch, arrowroot, and flour to thicken sauces and gravies, kudzu (along with potato starch and rice flour) has been the chief thickening agent for sauces in Asian cooking. Kudzu (or *kuzu*) is derived from the starchy root of a wild perennial vine considered a pest in areas such as the South, where it grows uncontrollably.

Kudzu is virtually tasteless and odorless and behaves similarly to cornstarch and arrowroot, yielding a sauce that is smooth and translucent. It is usually dissolved, then heated. It works at fairly low temperatures and, like cornstarch, should not be cooked much past the point where it thickens. In storage, kudzu may crystallize into lumps that must be pounded back to powder before it will dissolve properly. Macrobiotic cooks recommend the use of kudzu for its alkaline properties, balancing the acidity of certain ingredients. It is available in natural-foods stores and in Asian food stores. Store it as you would cornstarch. See Scallops and Shrimp with Black Bean Sauce (page 222) for a way to cook with kudzu.

Mirin

Mirin, once exclusively a beverage in Japan, is now one of the four essential flavorings along with miso, sake, and dashi stock (a stock made with dried fish) in the simple but elegant art of classic

Japanese cooking. This light golden syrupy sweet wine gives many dishes, including teriyaki, sukiyaki, yakitori, sushi rolls, and many dipping sauces, a nice flavor boost.

The Japanese brewmasters first made mirin hundreds of years ago by adding sweet rice to unfiltered sake, rendering a sweeter version of the latter. Eventually, a rice product called *shochu* revolutionized mirin to its present sweetly yeasty form. Explains John Schmidt from Eastern Sun Foods in North Carolina, "There are ninety mirin producers in Japan who make it mainly as a sideline to sake brewing. Only ten make mirin as a sole specialty and only two make authentic mirin." Checking the ingredients list on the mirin in my pantry, I indeed found the product to consist of water, sodium succinate, monosodium fumarate, monosodium glutamate, HPP, dextrose, starch syrup, ethanol, and mirin flavor, which John says add up to cornstarch, glucose, and pure ethyl alcohol. *Makawa*, distributed by Mitoku, he says is one of the authentic mirins available in this country, made by a natural distillation process using sweet rice and the *koji* mold (also used to age miso). Genuine mirin requires six months' maturation time.

The presence of alcohol and esters make this fermented product a natural taste enhancer. It is especially prized for neutralizing the strong smell of fish. Some cooks ignite the mirin before adding it to a dish to burn off the alcohol (which is less than 1 percent), so it will glaze cooked food and add a mild sweetness.

You can find the chemicalized mirin in any Japanese food store. Natural-foods stores are apt to have the mirin with more readable (and more wholesome) ingredients. Once you have opened it, refrigerate mirin for up to three months.

Sesame-Ginger Pork and Mushrooms

 *4 to 6 servings*

3 tablespoons peanut oil
1 pound boneless pork loin, trimmed and cut into 1½-inch
  strips
3 tablespoons sake
2 tablespoons mirin
2 tablespoons soy sauce
3 tablespoons minced ginger
½ pound fresh shiitake or button mushrooms, sliced
1 teaspoon Oriental sesame oil

1. Add 1 tablespoon peanut oil to a heated wok. Stir-fry pork
for about 3 minutes, until no longer pink. Remove from wok.
2. Add 2 tablespoons peanut oil to wok. Stir in sake, mirin,
soy sauce, and ginger and cook for 3 minutes. Stir in mushrooms
and cook for 2 minutes. Add pork to wok and stir-fry 1 minute.
Remove from heat and stir in sesame oil. Serve hot.

Miso

"Every Japanese—110 million—on the average consumes a few
spoonfuls [of miso] a day in one form or another," explains Shizuo
Tsuji in his book *Japanese Cooking* (Kodansha, 1980). Until recently, miso was well known in this country only with people who
shop in health-food stores and with those who follow macrobiotic
diets. Now those who share in the growing popularity of Japanese
cuisine know about miso as an important staple. Miso is a high-

protein paste, thick and spreadable like peanut butter and salty and beefy like soy sauce. It dissolves easily in hot liquid and is used more often in Japanese cooking to flavor thin broths or dipping sauces. It comes in a spectrum of earth colors from tan and rust to amber and chocolate brown, each embodying different flavors and aromas. Like soy sauce, miso is a fermented soy product, made from soybeans and a grain—rice or barley—that is soaked, then inoculated with a *koji* mold. Miso has a superior nutritional value, containing millions of beneficial bacteria in a rich mixture of oils, sugars, minerals, and amino acids. This savory paste contains a small amount of vitamin B_{12}, a nutrient almost never found in nonmeat sources. One tablespoon has about 30 calories and 25 grams of protein.

Miso can be used as a concentrated base to greatly enhance the taste and tint of soups and stocks. It can also flavor sauces, dips, dressings, and marinades for fish, poultry, meat, and vegetables. Mixed with peanut butter and other flavorings, it makes a great, nutritious sandwich spread. Dissolve miso in some of the hot liquid before adding it to soup toward the end of the cooking period. Never boil miso, as this destroys some of its beneficial organisms. Preserved with its high salt content, miso keeps indefinitely in an airtight container. Store it in the refrigerator.

Eggplant, Peas, and Miso

 *4 servings*

Serve this savory dish with rice or Oriental noodles.

1 medium-size eggplant (or 2 small Japanese eggplants)
¼ cup peanut or olive oil
1 cup fresh or frozen peas
3 cloves garlic, minced
2 tablespoons miso

1 tablespoon cold water
½ teaspoon Oriental sesame oil

1. Cut eggplant into small cubes. Sauté cubes in peanut or olive oil until lightly browned, about 10 minutes. Add peas and garlic, reduce heat, cover, and cook about 10 minutes more, stirring occasionally.

2. Combine miso with water and stir into vegetable mixture. Cook for 2 minutes over low heat. Stir in sesame oil and serve.

Sake

Sake, its sultry, yeasty, and full-bodied warmth once incorporated into Shinto religious ceremonies, is a national beverage in Japan, along with tea. You can invariably expect it at any Japanese meal, as an accompanying beverage or integral cooking component.

Sake is made by inoculating cooked rice with the mold koji, the same one used to ferment soybeans into the condiment miso. However, in contrast to miso, which may take as long as two years to age into a mellow, thick paste, sake is brewed and ready in just over two months. Unlike wine made from grapes, sake has no greater or lesser vintages. However, like wine, once exposed to air its bouquet and aroma dissipate within days.

Fragrant and colorless, the best sake is made from good-quality rice and pure spring water. Along with miso, dashi stock, and mirin, sake is one of the "gang of four" ingredients in Japanese cooking. It is used as a tenderizer the way Western cooking uses acid ingredients. It also balances out strong flavors and brings along delicate ones. It is used somewhat the way alcoholic beverages are used in Western cooking—in small quantities added near the end of cooking, just so the alcohol expires with the heating. Sake is found in any liquor store.

Sake-Marinated Chicken

 *4 servings*

2 pounds boned chicken breasts
¼ cup sake
¼ cup tamari soy sauce
4 teaspoons finely minced ginger
2 teaspoons finely minced garlic
2 tablespoons peanut oil

1. Cut chicken into 1-inch cubes (remove skin or leave on, as desired).
2. Mix remaining ingredients except peanut oil in a shallow bowl. Stir in chicken cubes and marinate for 30 minutes to 1 hour in refrigerator.
3. Heat wok, then add oil. Drain the marinade from the chicken and add chicken to wok. Cook over high heat, stirring frequently, until meat is cooked through, 10 to 15 minutes. Serve immediately.

Variations: Substitute firm-fleshed fish, such as monkfish, swordfish, or halibut, for the chicken. Or combine the chicken (or fish) with stir-fried vegetables, such as snow peas, red peppers, daikon, jicama, burdock, green beans, etc.

Tamari Soy Sauce

Tamari is a rich brown-black natural soy sauce, preferred to the rapidly manufactured Western soy sauce, which is made from acid-hydrolyzed protein, corn syrup, caramel coloring, monosodium glutamate, and preservatives. Tamari is just one variety of soy sauce; *shoyu* is another, similar-tasting one. However, tamari, unlike shoyu, uses no wheat in its fermentation process. The Japanese word *tamari* refers to the liquid accumulating during the miso fermentation process, but with Western marketing, the word has come to be applied differently here.

Amino acids created during tamari's fermentation of soy protein and the glutamic acid lend tamari its unique rich, beefy flavor. Tamari is used like the soy sauce we've known for years—in Chinese, Japanese, and other Asian cuisines—but its flavor is more intense and authentic than the ersatz product. Tamari will keep indefinitely, stored at room temperature.

Note: Use tamari for any recipe in this book—and any other—calling for soy sauce.

Umeboshi Plum

My first knowledge of this reddish-pink pickled plum came from a friend who was heavily into a macrobiotic diet. She recommended the shriveled salty condiment as an antidote to hangovers. The alkalinity of the plum supposedly would restore the system to its proper pH balance, which was offset by the excess of alcohol. I found a more reliable remedy for hangovers was not to drink too much.

Fantastic cures aside, the Japanese do regard the umeboshi as a digestive aid that works best if taken in the morning. Native to Japan, umeboshi is made from green plums that resemble apricots. The fruit is marinated in a salty vinegar brine along with leaves from the shiso plant, a member of the mint family. Umeboshi is available as the cured plum with a seed about the size of an olive pit, or it may be sold pitted and mashed as a plum paste. One popular way to consume salty-sour umeboshi is as the center of rice balls seasoned with sesame seeds and sometimes seaweed. Umeboshi are expensive and available mainly in Japanese or natural-foods stores. See the umeboshi variation on the Cucumber Sushi Rolls recipe, page 237.

Wasabi

If you are in any way an habitué of sushi bars, you are no doubt familiar with the Japanese green mustard called *wasabi*, which is more like horseradish than mustard, though the two are not related. Wasabi comes from the root of a plant that thrives in the swampy cold areas near rivers. Its smoldering pungency and cleansing fragrance are needed only in small amounts and, along with the soy dipping sauce, it is integral to the sushi experience. Since wasabi does not grow much outside of Japan, the root is usually available in the West as a paste or as a powder that can be reconstituted with water. Wasabi is available in Japanese food stores and in some natural-foods stores. Store the paste as you would mustard, and the powder with dry goods. See Cucumber Sushi Rolls, page 237, for a recipe using wasabi.

SEA VEGETABLES

Asian cookery is no doubt most responsible for the assimilation
of the various seaweeds, or sea vegetables, into our diet. The
Japanese and other Eastern cultures have been much more re-
sourceful in plumbing life from the sea than have we in the West.
To many Westerners this stuff that the relentless tides blithely
wash ashore seems about as appetizing as a piece of driftwood. The
Japanese know otherwise. Few cuisines are more simple and elegant
than that of the Japanese, who have infused various forms of life
from the sea into many delicious dishes.

An important reason for farming the sea for more than its fish
is for its nutritious vegetable matter, unmatched by that grown
on land. Most seaweeds are complex carbohydrates that include
a small amount of protein and fat and some vitamins. But their
most notable contribution as a food source is in the mineral department. They are generally abundant in iodine, with traces of
many other minerals, including the ever-important calcium, mag-
nesium, and phosphorus. The Japanese flavor the foundation of
much of their cooking, dashi stock, as well as other broths, soups,
and salads, with kombu seaweed. And, of course, you may have
eaten seaweed as part of sushi, vinegared rice rolls that accompany
sashimi, the delectable raw fish.

Seaweed is used in other parts of the world too. The Welsh,

Irish, English, French, and Hawaiians make use of seaweed in baking and cooking. In New England, dulse (a red seaweed) is harvested and has long been eaten there.

The following seaweeds are available dried in Japanese food stores and also in natural-foods stores. Before they are reconstituted, they last indefinitely (they will increase their volume from two to four times when rehydrated). Store them in a dark, dry spot.

Arame This seaweed, from the southern coastal regions of Japan, looks like charcoal-black fronds suspended in a wavy ripple when dried. Arame needs just a 3-to-5-minute soak in water to revive it for use in soups, stir-fries, on sandwiches. It is mild-flavored and blends well with tomato, curry, and ginger-garlic seasonings.

Dulse Dulse is perhaps the only seaweed some Americans, especially those near Atlantic and Pacific coastal waters, have eaten. It has thin fronds that seem to wave like the hand of a poltergeist, but its flavor is quite earthy and spinachlike. Relishes and salads have been a popular receptacle for its briny flavor, as have a savory tea biscuit. Dried dulse softens in liquid in about 7 minutes. It works well in salads, soups, stews, stuffings, with any vegetables, and as a garnish for seafood.

Hijiki Looking like a tangled mop of ebony yarn, hijiki (or *hiziki*) is one of the most calcium-rich of the sea vegetables. It is indigenous to the low rocky waters of coastal Japan. Its thin curling strands need about 15 minutes of rehydration. Hijiki is one of the most briny of the seaweeds, adding a true seaside character with some beany notes to foods. Its limp fronds can be a garnish to fish or salads with strong-flavored ingredients. It marries nicely with meaty-flavored mushrooms and sweet carrots or red peppers.

Kelp Kelp thrives on the Pacific coast and is available in a granular form. It is most often used as a condiment for seafood, poultry, or meat, for grain dishes or vegetable medleys. Kelp is sometimes used instead of salt, even though it is also high in sodium.

Kombu Drawn from Pacific coastal waters, kombu is sold as dried wide flat strips that must be soaked for about 10 minutes to reconstitute. Kombu, from the Laminaria family, is a deep sea-brown color. Along with bonito flakes, it flavors the Japanese dashi stock. About 1 ounce of dried kombu is added to each quart of water as a seasoning for the stock, releasing flavor and adding a slight thickness. It should not be overcooked or its briny flavor will turn unpleasantly bitter.

Nori (Laver) Nori is farmed from the rocky coastal waters of the southernmost islands of Japan and from both coasts of the United States. The parchmentlike sheets of olive-black are the famous wrapping enfolding the delicious vinegared rice in sushi rolls. Nori is from the *Porphyra* genus of marine algae. This crisp alga is always toasted over an open flame to improve its sea flavor and fragrance and its firm texture. Nori has other uses in Japanese cuisine—as a garnish, a flavoring for vegetables, crumbled over rice dishes.

Wakame Wakame, a member of the brown algae family, is fished from the waters around the islands of Japan. When rehydrated—in about 3 minutes—the frond's spine may be very firm and need to be trimmed off. Wakame is used to season soups and in leafy green salads with a light vinaigrette. It has a mild bean-corn flavor that goes well with other fresh vegetables.

Sea and Land Vegetable Soup

 *6 to 8 servings*

Don't be dismayed by all the "health foods" in this soup. It is a rich-tasting, filling soup, great for a cold winter day with a salad, bread, and nothing else. You can find sunflower seed butter at most natural-foods stores. You can also grind your own or use all peanut butter.

2 tablespoons peanut oil
1 large onion, chopped
4 cloves garlic, minced
2 large potatoes, cut into large dice
4 carrots, sliced
2 teaspoons Garam Masala (see page 201)
5 cups vegetable or meat stock
$^1/_2$ cup sunflower seed butter
2 tablespoons peanut butter
$1^1/_2$ cups fresh or frozen peas
1 cup arame (or hijiki)
3 tablespoons miso

1. Heat oil in a large pot. Add onion, garlic, potatoes, carrots, and Garam Masala and cook 7 minutes. Add stock and bring to a boil. Lower to a simmer.

2. Combine nut butters in a bowl. Add some hot soup liquid and stir until well dissolved. Stir back into soup.

3. Add peas and seaweed. Cook another 10 to 15 minutes, until potatoes are tender.

4. Dissolve miso with some of the hot broth in a small bowl and return to soup pot. Serve hot.

Variation: Add 1 cup cooked chick-peas or cooked dried beans.

Dulse-Thyme Scones

Makes about 1 $^1/_2$ dozen

$^1/_2$ cup dried dulse
2 cups unbleached white flour

2 teaspoons sugar
3 teaspoons baking powder
2 teaspoons fresh thyme, or ½ teaspoon dried
¼ teaspoon salt
4 tablespoons butter
1 egg, beaten
⅔ cup milk

1. Cover dulse with water and soak for about 10 minutes. Rinse, drain, and chop coarsely.

2. Preheat oven to 400°F. Mix flour, sugar, baking powder, thyme, and salt in a bowl. Cut in butter until mixture has the texture of oatmeal.

3. Stir in the dulse. Add the egg and milk and stir just until flour is absorbed. Knead dough on a floured surface for about 1 minute. Shape into flattened balls about 3 inches in diameter. Place on oiled baking sheet and bake until golden brown, 12 to 15 minutes.

Low-Sodium Herbal Seasoning with Kelp

 *Makes about ⅓ cup*

2 teaspoons kelp
½ teaspoon garlic powder
2 teaspoons dried parsley
½ teaspoon dried thyme
½ teaspoon dried marjoram
2 tablespoons toasted sesame seeds, crushed
⅛ teaspoon cayenne pepper
½ teaspoon celery seed, crushed
½ teaspoon fennel seed, crushed
1 teaspoon salt (optional)

Combine all ingredients in an airtight jar. Use instead of salt on all foods and in cooking.

Wakame-Chervil Omelet

 *1 or 2 servings*

1 2-inch piece dried wakame
2 scallions, sliced
3 eggs
2 tablespoons chopped fresh chervil
2 tablespoons butter

1. Soak wakame in water for 15 minutes, until soft. Drain, cut away tough rib, and chop coarsely.
2. Combine wakame, scallions, eggs, and chervil in a bowl. Beat well.
3. Melt butter in a skillet. Pour in egg mixture. Cook just until set near edges. Flip two sides inward and flip omelet over to cook through. Serve hot, with sliced tomatoes if desired.

Cucumber Sushi Rolls

 *4 servings*

2 cups short-grain rice
2¾ cups water
1 3-inch piece kombu
3 tablespoons rice vinegar
1 tablespoon sugar
1 teaspoon salt

2 sheets nori
Vinegar-water (1 cup water combined with 1 teaspoon vinegar)
  for hands
1 tablespoon prepared wasabi
1 cucumber, peeled, seeded, and sliced lengthwise into thin
  strips

1. Combine rice, water, and kombu in a heavy-bottom pot. Cover pot, bring to a boil, then remove and discard kombu. Turn heat down and cook, covered, until water is absorbed, about 15 minutes. Remove from heat.

2. Heat vinegar, sugar, and salt in a small saucepan, just until sugar dissolves. Set aside to cool.

3. Toss rice with vinegar mixture, using a wooden spoon to coat all grains.

4. Toast nori by holding over a flame for a few seconds. Moisten hands with vinegar-water. Spread about ⅔ cup rice over the lower three-quarters of the nori, leaving an uncovered edge about 1 inch wide along the top edge.

5. Spread a thin line of wasabi across the center of rice. Place 3 to 4 cucumber strips along the wasabi. Roll up toward the uncovered edge of nori. Moisten edge and finish rolling. Squeeze gently to seal. Slice roll with a very sharp wet knife into 5 to 6 rolls. Repeat process with each nori sheet.

CUCUMBER SUSHI WITH UMEBOSHI: Instead of wasabi, spread a thin layer of umeboshi paste along the center of rice.

VEGETABLE SUSHI: Add strips of cooked carrot along with cucumber to rolls.

Agar

Agar (also called *agar-agar*) is the gelatinous extract of the red alga seaweed called *tengusa* in Malay (meaning "heavenly grass"). Used as a jelling or stabilizing agent in foods, much the way gelatin is, it is often found in commercially made health foods in this country. It is also the jelling agent of choice in Japanese and other Asian cooking. People who eschew animal-derived products of any sort opt for agar, since gelatin is the protein extract of animal bones. (You may also remember agar from biology class—it served as a sterile culture medium for organisms gathered for study.)

Agar's firming properties have been used for ages in Asian cooking—in sweets, confections, and for giving structure to savory molds and cold salads. It is used the same way as gelatin, but it sets at a higher temperature. It is more fragile when molded than gelatin, but less inclined to rubberiness. About 2 to 3 tablespoons of agar flakes, softened first in a little cold water, will thicken 3 to 4 cups of liquid. As with gelatin, you should chill the agar mixture until it is slightly thickened but not set before adding ingredients you wish to suspend in its final glassiness.

Agar, rich in iron, potassium, and some trace minerals, is usually available in flakes resembling thin shavings of clear paraffin, or in threads, or in long strips known as *kanten*. Some Chinese cooks soak the kanten in cold water to soften it, and then serve it as a cold soy-seasoned appetizer. You can find agar in most health-food stores and in Oriental food stores.

Couscous Pudding with Date-Raisin Sauce

 *4 servings*

Although the other ingredients are not particularly Asian, this is one way Asian cuisine would use agar—as a thickener in a dessert.

1 cup couscous
3 cups water
1/4 cup sugar
2/3 cup chopped walnuts
2 teaspoons vanilla extract
1 teaspoon orange zest
1 cup pitted dates
1/2 cup raisins
1/2 teaspoon cinnamon
1 tablespoon agar flakes
1 1/2 cups apple juice

1. Combine couscous, water, sugar, nuts, vanilla, and zest in a saucepan. Simmer covered for about 10 minutes, until liquid is absorbed. Pour into a 9-inch-square dish or 4 individual dessert bowls. Chill.

2. *Make sauce*: Combine dates, raisins, cinnamon, agar, and apple juice in a saucepan. Simmer for 5 minutes, stirring. Refrigerate sauce until set. Whip in a blender or food processor until creamy. Serve chilled pudding topped with sauce and whipped cream, if desired.

INDEX